How To Spot A Fox

How To Spot A Fox

J. David Henry

Chapters Publishing Ltd., Shelburne, Vermont 05482

Published by
Chapters Publishing Ltd.
2031 Shelburne Road
Shelburne, Vermont 05482

Library of Congress Cataloguing-in-Publication Data

Henry, J. David
    How to spot a fox / J. David Henry
        p.   cm. (The How to spot series)
    Includes bibliographical references (p.) and index.
    ISBN 1-881527-18-2 (hardcover) : $21.95. —
    ISBN 1-881527-17-4 (softcover) : $12.95
    1. Red fox. 2. Red fox — Behavior. 3. Wildlife watching.
I. Title. II. Series.
QL737.C22H45 1993
599.74'442—dc20

93-24091
CIP

Trade distribution by
Firefly Books Ltd.
250 Sparks Avenue
Willowdale, Ontario
Canada M2H 2S4

Printed and bound in Canada by
Metropole Litho
St. Bruno de Montarville, Québec

Designed by Impress, Inc. / Northampton, Massachusetts

Cover photograph by Darrell Gulin / AllStock

To the memory
of my father,
Daniel J. Henry,
with appreciation
for unspoken wisdom
communicated gently.

Contents

INTRODUCTION

The Prince and The Raven

I T WAS A SPARKLING, sun-saturated autumn afternoon in the Northern woods, warm enough to make me think summer was revisiting the land. The wind was beating the lake into a frenzy. I looked up into the crowns of the aspen trees above me, where lemon-colored leaves were dancing.

All morning I had been following The Prince, a young male red fox, through the forest of Saskatchewan's Prince Albert National Park. Off and on for several weeks, I had been observing the behavior of this yearling dog fox closely. The Prince was now honoring a tradition I had seen in other foxes: during the warmest part of an autumn afternoon, he napped. He had had a fine morning hunting mice in the tall grasses that grow next to certain hiking trails in the park, and he had buried several

---

Alert, cunning and ever-watchful, red foxes can nonetheless be observed and studied if approached correctly.

of these "trophies" in shallow holes, scattering his caches around his territory for future use.

The Prince selected a sunny ridge, sheltered from the wind. He curled around himself twice, lay down and licked his front legs and paws in preparation for his nap. On the other side of the small forest opening, I turned off the tape recorder I used to collect field notes and lay down on the colorful, freshly fallen leaves, with a birch log as a pillow. As I settled a few yards away from the fox, I thought, "What eminently good timing this creature has."

Just then, a raven coasted overhead, slicing the onshore breeze like a kite. It squawked as it flew over the fox and human below. Then the shiny black scavenger landed on top of a nearby black spruce and wobbled back and forth until it gained its balance. The fox looked up at the bird for a moment and merely yawned.

From years of studying free-ranging foxes, I knew that foxes and ravens usually have an unfriendly, somewhat competitive relationship. For example, a raven will follow a red fox that is carrying food. The raven flies along, trailing the fox at a distance, trying to observe where the fox buries the food so that it can pilfer the cache once the fox leaves. If the fox detects the bird, it counters by continuing to trot along through the forest until the bird gives up in discouragement. I have also seen foxes flash their teeth and make other threatening displays at ravens and crows.

I looked back at The Prince. He put his head down and began to nap. The raven rode the wind-tossed treetop for a minute or so, then launched himself off the spruce, floated down and landed softly on the ground. The bird remained a safe distance away from the fox. The fox kept his head down but opened one eye and peered. For a minute, there was only silence and glances. Then the raven, in an excited, floating hop that is so characteristic of the bird, started to zigzag its way toward the resting fox. The fox raised its head. The raven stopped, lowered itself slightly and gave a soft croak. The fox glanced at me, then back at the bird. Finally, the fox yawned and put its head back down while keeping its eyes on the raven. "What the devil is going on?" I thought to myself, and tried to remain as relaxed as possible. I even feigned sleep, keeping one eye slightly opened.

Slowly, the raven zigzagged its way toward the fox, sometimes backtracking a step or two, watching the fox carefully and then moving forward again. The bird continued this bizarre dance for two or three minutes, slowly making its way closer to the fox. It finally settled down just a yard from the fox's side, like a hen taking to her nest. The bird preened a few feathers on its chest, then lowered its head and closed its eyes. The Prince, who had his head down but was watching the bird all this time, now lifted his head and looked around as if puzzled. He gazed intently at the sleeping raven, then over at me, then up into the aspen. Over the next couple of minutes, he slowly closed and opened his eyes several times, looking at the bird each time, and then, as if he had reached a decision, he stretched out on his side in the warm sunlight and slept.

By this point I seemed to be the only one there who was bothered by insomnia. "What is going on? A fox and a raven napping together?" I thought to myself. A fox and its potential prey sharing the warmth of a September afternoon? It wasn't the size of the opening in the forest that dictated what I was observing. The opening was large enough to accommodate a herd of elk. There were hundreds of sunny openings within easy reach of the raven. Yet the scavenger and the predator slept peacefully, almost within touching distance of each other, as if the warmth and beauty of the autumn afternoon, which had temporarily suspended the coming of winter, had also temporarily suspended their normally competitive relationship.

After 20 minutes or so, The Prince ended the siesta as casually as it had begun. At first, he opened both eyes and, without

With an unmistakably catlike stretch, this red fox rouses itself from a midday nap.

moving, stared curiously at the sleeping raven. Then, still on his side, he began to stretch. In the process, he scratched one forepaw against the ground. The raven catapulted out of sleep in an awkward hop that moved it a little farther away from the fox. As the bird strutted back and forth, parallel to the fox, each observed the other in calm, but tense, curiosity. The mood had changed between the two. The truce was over. The fox finally rose up on its feet and stretched in a deep, catlike bow—hips high, chest and chin on the ground and forelegs stretched out in front. At the end of the stretch, the fox stood and turned slightly to-

ward the raven. The raven looked back. The bird squawked, hopped twice, lifted off, and soon disappeared over the treetops. The Prince, as if nothing unusual had happened, turned and trotted into the flickering sunlight of the aspen woods to begin an afternoon and evening of hunting and scavenging.

What relationship these two animals had, I shall never know. What was the meaning of this exchange? I had never observed anything like this before, and I have never seen it again. Yet for one brief moment, fox and raven napped side by side, completely accepting one another. What communication occurred between the raven and The Prince on that sunny ridge? What nonverbal thoughts passed through their avian and carnivore brains? For every question that a field biologist can answer about the animals that he or she is studying, a hundred more elude one's grasp. During all my years of research, I had never before observed a fox and raven napping together. Perhaps for these animals it was not even an unusual encounter. But I have been wondering about it ever since.

This book attempts to give you the skills to get started as a wildlife observer, to become a good field biologist. It won't be easy. It will demand patience and perseverance. But if you have the commitment and the dedication, it can be done. I did not come upon this encounter between The Prince and the raven quickly or easily. On and off for 14 years of my life, I have observed red foxes. I have had to cope with many obstacles—the reality of doing field research on free-ranging wildlife. Remember, too, that you do not have to move to a wilderness area to study wildlife; some of the greatest research in ethology (the science of animal behavior) has been carried out by observing animals that you can find in your own backyard.

In this book are the tools to get around some of the obstacles you will meet. The first chapter discusses where you might find red foxes and how to interpret their field signs. But locating the fox is just the first step. The second chapter examines what we understand about how the world of the red fox fits together. The third chapter stands back and looks at the fox. It explains why the red fox has evolved to look the way it does. Chapters four and five explore the red fox as hunter. Foxes also obtain food by scavenging, and any surplus food is cached for the fox's future use. Chapters six and seven explore some of the surprising elements of these seemingly simple behaviors. Chapter eight focuses on fox conservation. It examines why some fox species are doing well in their association with humans while other fox species, the swift fox for example, are endangered.

Wildlife management is increasingly becoming a team effort—projects are organized by scientists from different disciplines teamed up with interested citizens, all coordinating their efforts to achieve a clear, well-defined conservation goal. In the last chapter of this book, I introduce some of the types of skills a person needs if he or she wishes to work on wildlife ecology and endangered species conservation projects of the future.

I encourage you to observe foxes, and I wish you good luck in your efforts to do so. In the field, you may make valuable observations on their behaviors or gain new insights into their ecology. I hope you will share your most important findings with me. I know you will inevitably encounter many frustrations. Use your imagination and intelligence in solving each of your field problems. And persist. That is most important.

You will eventually witness tragic events, some man-caused and some natural, that are inflicted on wild animals. In addition to carrying out your field observation, also consider joining an environmental organization. Become an active, participating member and work for the better protection of all wildlife.

But if you persist in your efforts to study wild foxes, you will be given moments that you will cherish for the rest of your life. Enjoy these moments, they are immensely valuable gifts, and you will certainly have earned them.

— *J. David Henry*
Prince Albert National Park
Waskesiu Lake
Saskatchewan, Canada

I

Where to Find Foxes

THE RED FOX has been amazingly successful. It now has the largest geographical range of any living carnivore (flesh-eating mammal) and continues to expand its range: across the tundra of northern Canada and Siberia; in Australia, where British settlers introduced it for fox-hunting purposes in the mid-1800s; and across the arid regions of the Middle East and northern Africa. In studying the red fox, we are studying one of the real success stories of the dog family, Canidae (KAN-i-dee). The red fox is a canid species that is adaptable, intelligent and highly evolved. To understand its society is to enter an intriguing foreign culture. Such a foreign adventure, even if your animals live within a neighboring woodlot, can greatly expand your perception of the world. This book is an attempt to explore the culture of the fox, principally that of the red fox (*Vulpes vulpes*).

Red fox society, just like human society, has evolved over the span of millions of years. Its present characteristics are the result of biological evolution—the slow sculpturing of the fox's adaptations to match its environments. The behavior of the red fox is also the result of individual learning, combined with animal traditions passed down from parent to offspring. In many ways, then, the evolution of red fox society is not that different from our own.

To study red foxes, you first have to find them, and this can be a considerable challenge. Foxes will normally spot you before you spot them. They are animals of keen

Foxes can attain running speeds of up to 45 mph, faster than wolves, coyotes and many dogs.

Keen vision, hearing and smell enable foxes to spot you before you spot them.

vision, hearing and smell, and can escape at considerable speed. Over the years, I have observed a number of chases between foxes and other wild canids, and in these contests, the red fox was always able to outrun and outdodge pursuing coyotes, wolves or dogs as large as Doberman pinschers. The well-known biologist Milton Hildebrand recorded red foxes attaining speeds of up to 45 mph (72 kph) over short distances, making the red fox only marginally slower than the cheetah. In fact, it is one of the fastest sprinters in the entire mammal family.

Given these characteristics, it is not surprising that you usually will be able to ob-serve foxes only when they choose to be watched. This book will explore where to search in order to find them, but even more important, it will tell you how to act around red foxes so that you might be tolerated by them. Once you have learned this basic "fox etiquette," your chances of being able to ob-serve them for long periods will increase significantly.

Let's start by examining how you might determine whether foxes exist on your fam-ily farm or near your home or cottage. Then we will discuss how you should attempt to study them. Because foxes are so adapt-able—changing their behaviors to cope with specific circumstances—it is impossible to have just one plan for studying them. I can tell you what works for me, but you will have to get out and see what works in your area. It is most important to observe the way the foxes respond to you. By doing so, you will discover clues about which technique to try next.

Red foxes can show a wide range of reactions to humans. In places where they are hunted or trapped, they can be extremely shy and difficult to observe. Where foxes are protected from hunting and trapping, as they are in parks and other nature reserves,

The red fox has evolved into an adaptable and flexible species, at home in an impressive array of habitats—even urban areas.

they may eventually lose most of their natural fear of man and become easier to watch. Most of the red fox research that I have carried out has been done in Prince Albert National Park in northern Saskatchewan. The foxes in this park have been protected from hunting and trapping for over 50 years. Many park visitors believe the foxes are tame because they often see them scavenging in campgrounds, hunting along roadsides or traveling along beaches and hiking trails. However, the foxes are highly selective in their "tame" reaction to humans. I have found that they accept me only in certain areas where they are accustomed to encountering humans, but they react with alarm and fright when I try to observe them away from the campgrounds and roads.

It normally takes a week or more of patient, demanding work to get a fox to accept me so that I can travel behind it through the woods and observe its natural behavior. To accomplish this, each time I encounter a wild fox, I put a small piece of meat on the ground. Usually the animal comes over and eats it. I want the foxes to learn that if they find me, they get a food reward. That is the only time I feed a fox, because I also want it to learn that after that initial treat, it is pointless to wait for more. Some foxes are very adept at learning this lesson, and some are extremely slow. Sometimes a fox and I, both totally

Trotting along a path, this fox hunts for mice, voles or other small burrowing mammals.

bored, will spend hours just standing or sitting around looking at each other until the fox catches on to "the rules of the game."

The next lesson I want the foxes to learn is that I represent no danger if they permit me to follow quietly behind them as they hunt and scavenge. When I first began, the foxes often fled and I chased after them. All I accomplished by doing so was to scare the fox even more and bruise myself by crashing through bushes. Soon I learned that if the fox runs away, simply let it go. But I always hang around the area for a couple of hours, or I come back over the next couple of days. If the fox finds me again, I give it another small piece of meat, and we begin the cycle all over again. After a week or so of this tac-

tic, the fox often chooses to allow me to follow it, first for a few minutes, then slowly for part of an hour or more. It is always the fox's choice, and the only thing I can do is follow a hundred yards or so behind it, careful not to bother the animal, trying to make as little noise as possible and being particularly still when the fox is hunting. I become as predictable and dull in my behavior as possible so that the fox gradually chooses to ignore me and sets about its business.

I can never predict how long a fox will choose to allow me to follow it, and often I cannot tell whether we accidentally become separated or whether the fox has ditched me. Overall, it is a good system. On several days, I was able to follow the same fox—and

Red foxes do best in half-open country of mixed forest and field, hunting in so-called "edge" environments.

ible species. It can live in an impressive array of habitats. It exists on tundra far north of the treeline, in many different types of forests, in the semi-arid grassland regions of the American West and on the steppes of Russia and Mongolia. However, there is a limit to the dryness that red foxes can tolerate. They do not inhabit the Sahara, Mojave and other desert regions of the world.

Humans have produced many drastic changes to landscapes, and these alterations have proved harmful to many wildlife species. The red fox, however, is an exception to this pattern. In general, red foxes have thrived in their association with man. Foxes live on golf courses and in city parks and ravines. But the adaptability of the red fox does not stop there. David Macdonald, a British researcher, has documented several generations of foxes being raised in a warehouse on the outskirts of London. Stephen Harris, another British fox researcher, has studied foxes in a number of suburbs in Britain, showing that their main food sources were earthworms harvested off people's lawns at night, garden produce, and the food they could pilfer from dustbins or garbage pails.

To determine whether foxes exist in your area, you have to begin searching for clues. The first sign to learn to identify is red fox tracks. If you are lucky enough to live in an

see everything it did—for 11 hours.

There are no guarantees in this business of fox watching. I remember one young man who came to the park to study how foxes raise their young. He did everything right and exhibited Herculean patience, but after more than 700 hours of quietly observing from a blind at various dens, he had a total of 90 seconds of actually seeing red foxes. It is always the foxes that determine if a person will be allowed to study them, and if they choose "no," there is very little you can do about it.

Interpreting field signs

How do you go about establishing where red foxes live in your area? The red fox has evolved into an adaptable and flex-

area that is snow-covered for part of the winter, the opportunities for detecting fox tracks greatly increase. If you do not have snow, or you are looking for fox tracks during the warm months, then you must rely on muddy patches of ground or wet sandy areas along beaches or creeks.

Spots that are always muddy can be very useful for detecting tracks. Or you may create muddy areas of your own. Search for places where animals funnel through small openings in a hedgerow or fence. Often these places are indicated by a well-worn path leading up to them or by bits of fur caught on the boards, branches or barbed wire of a fence. Pour water on the ground there and, with a tool, work it into a nice smooth mud. Wear gloves while doing this to reduce your scent to a minimum. Keep the site moist for a week or two, visiting it every couple of days, and see what animal tracks appear.

If you are trying to spot fox tracks in snow, there are a few things to keep in mind. If the snow of your area will support the weight of a fox, the animals will travel everywhere. But red foxes, like many other animals, are reluctant to wallow or hop through deep, fluffy snow, even for a short distance. It uses up too much energy. In my area, if there has been a snowstorm that has put 8 inches (20 cm) or more of new snow on the ground, red foxes "lie up" somewhere and become inactive for two or three days. Once

A good place to search for fox tracks is in an area of mud or moist sand, *top*. Fresh snow cover, *bottom*, clearly shows the tracks left by a fox *(left)*, a human *(center)* and a wolf *(right)*.

other animals (like snowshoe hares, squirrels, deer and elk) have moved around and made packed trails in the soft snow, foxes begin to roam again, using these tracks and trails almost exclusively. These conditions make for difficult tracking. Fox tracks

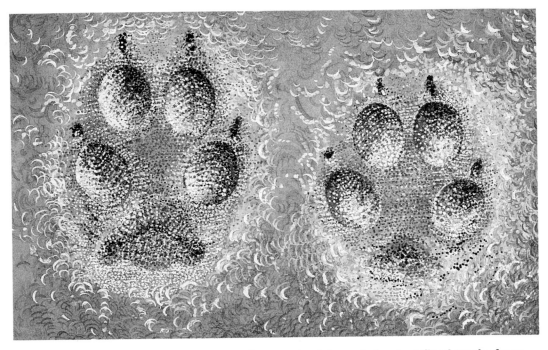

This life-sized illustration shows the small toe-pad prints and clearly defined marks from sharp, pointed claws typical of fox tracks. The forefoot of a fox is larger than the hind.

mixed in with other animal tracks can be hard to identify and may not be preserved for long. Foxes also like to walk along the edge of a plowed road or in tire tracks instead of lunging through softer, deeper snow next to the road.

Ideal winter tracking conditions are when you have 2 inches (5 cm) of fresh snow over a firm base. Foxes will be active and moving a great deal, and you should make the most of these conditions in searching out foxes in your area.

How do you identify the tracks of a red fox? Make a list of the canid and feline (cat family) species that exist in your area. For much of North America, this list will include coyotes and perhaps bobcats. For Northern areas, it may include wolf, lynx and even cougar. Don't forget to add the domestic dog and the house cat. Once you have this list, it will encompass all the carnivores that exhibit four toe pads and a heel pad in well-preserved tracks.

Now let's say you're looking down at a clear line of tracks left on a muddy trail. How do you tell if they are fox tracks? First, determine if they were made by a feline or canid species. Feline tracks usually do not show any claw marks, because most cat species have retractile claws. If your set of tracks exhibits four toe pads on each foot, and if claw marks are also present, you know for certain that you are dealing with a canid species. Unfortunately, domestic dogs come in a variety of sizes and body weights. This complicates matters. Red fox tracks are doglike in their appearance; they are smallish and fairly oval in shape, approximately 2 inches (5 cm) in diameter, although this may increase or decrease with the size of the fox and the softness of the surface. The forefoot of the fox is slightly larger and splays out more than the hind foot.

I wish I could tell you that fox tracks come with an indisputable identifying characteristic, but they don't. All that I can offer is a set of characteristics that would suggest that the tracks in front of you may well be the tracks of a red fox:

Toe pads in a fox track are often small, no bigger than the toe pads of a domestic cat; however, the sharp, pointy claws that are usually present in fox tracks clearly separate them from cat tracks. Furthermore, red foxes are animals of exquisite balance so that in certain gaits, fox tracks line up in almost a single line. Dog or coyote tracks tend to be in double file.

Another important characteristic to consider is the body weight of foxes compared to that of most domestic dogs or coyotes. If the tracks of the dog, young coyote and red fox are all the same size, the red fox would weigh approximately half as much as the dog or coyote. Red foxes have evolved to become very light-bodied animals for their size. With

practice, this difference in weight can be detected in tracks and used for separating dog and coyote tracks from fox tracks. Often when I am tracking, I carry a stick that is two inches (5 cm) in diameter, and I penetrate the snow or mud several times next to the track to develop a feeling for how much force is needed to make a track of the depth that I am examining. By doing this a number of times, I can often decide whether I

At certain gaits, fox tracks line up in almost a single line, *above.* **Dog and coyote tracks often tend to be double-file.**

am examining tracks left by a heavy-bodied dog or coyote, or by a light-bodied red fox. This sounds more complicated than it is. Try it, and I think you will find it can be helpful.

In my area of northern Saskatchewan, I have also found that the width of the track is a useful indicator in separating the tracks of red foxes from coyotes. In the snow, coyote tracks are wide enough that I can bend my first three fingers at the knuckles and slide them into the track. Red fox tracks

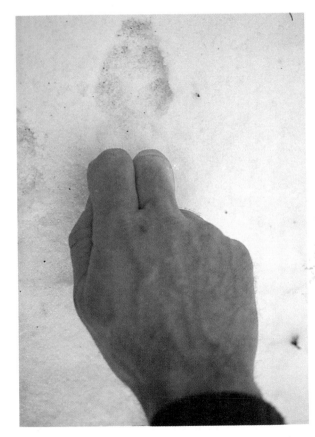

The author's "two-finger rule" allows him to determine that a track was left by a fox. Coyote tracks will accommodate three fingers.

will accommodate only my first two fingers. This two-or-three finger rule is taken along with the other evidence, and all of it is integrated to try to make a decision about whether I am looking at the track of a red fox or a coyote. Your hand may be a different size than mine and your wild canids may be a different size, but with practice, you can develop a rule that is reliable for your area.

The last field signs involve the fox's elimination products, urine and feces.

Urine marks can be identified by their color and, during part of the year, by their odor. The first thing to look at in identifying a urine mark is the quantity. Foxes release small "token" urine marks. If the volume is substantial, it probably isn't from a fox. Second, look at the color of the urine. Fox urine marks in snow usually have a light amber color; the urine marks of other canids are darker, more of a brownish amber hue. But be careful. The urine marks of all canids, including foxes, turn more brownish over time. Still, when you spot a small urine mark in the snow that has a light straw, amber color to it, there's a good chance that it is the urine mark of a fox.

Even more than other canid species, red foxes do a great deal of urine marking in their home areas. I have observed individual foxes making marks up to 70 times per hour while scavenging. I have observed only one or two of them empty the entire contents of their bladder at one squatting. In both

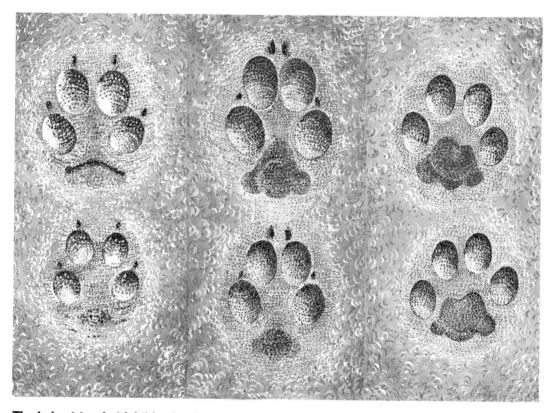

The bobcat track *(right)* is clearly delineated from the fox track *(left)* and the coyote track *(center)* because of the absence of claw marks. Coyote tracks are wider than foxes'.

cases, this occurred when a young fox was trespassing on another fox's territory.

But it is the odor of the fox's urine marks that really sets them apart. During the second half of winter, the urine marks of a red fox exhibit a definite "skunky" smell. These skunky urine marks can be smelled at several hundred yards. All you have to do is to learn to recognize the odor. Even this task is not difficult. Make a visit to a zoo or game farm during late January, and the pens or cages with captive red foxes will give you ample opportunity to become acquainted with the smell. In fact, just spend an hour standing near one of these pens and your clothes will give you a "take home" sample that is sure to raise comments. Once you are on to it, this midwinter fox odor is a valuable field sign.

It is perfectly safe to put your nose within 4 to 6 inches (10 to 15 cm) of a fox urine mark and smell for the characteristic odor. Droppings, or scats, however, are a completely different matter and should be examined and handled with extreme care. If the fox has any intestinal parasites, the eggs of the parasites will be in the scats and can infect other animals, including humans.

During a quiet moment, a red fox gazes into the calm waters of a northern lake.

One of the most dangerous of these parasites is the intestinal tapeworm *Echinococcus granulosus.* By far the best rule is: Do not handle or put your face close to the scats. Canid biologists normally carry plastic bags with them; when they find a scat, they turn a bag inside out over one hand, pick up the scat, invert the bag and tie it shut. If you use this technique, be sure that the bag does not have any holes. Once the scat is inside a completely sealed plastic bag, it is safe to examine. In a laboratory, canid scats are soaked in formaldehyde to kill the parasite eggs, and then a researcher examines them for food remnants under a ventilating hood, wearing a surgical mask and gloves.

The droppings vary in size depending upon the quantity and types of food the fox has eaten. On average, fox scats are 2.5 inches (6.4 cm) long and fairly slender. Coyote scats average 4 inches (10 cm) in length and are bulkier, but there is some overlap between the two species.

It is often possible—from a safe distance—to separate the scats of domestic dogs from those of foxes, coyotes and wolves. The scats of wild canids often have a high content of hair and bone chips, which is absent or limited in the scats of domestic dogs. If a scat is filled with bone chips or bone powder, it has a dirty white appearance. If the hair content in the scat is high, it has a slightly twisted end. Wild canid scats can be as variable as their diet. In my northern area during late summer, I often find red fox and coyote scats that are almost navy blue in color. These scats are composed almost completely of the undigested skins of wild blueberries. In England, David Macdonald describes fox scats entirely composed of soil and the soft scales of earthworms. And foxes feeding on garbage create scats that take on the look of domestic dog droppings.

Barks and shrieks

FOXES MAKE SEVERAL long-distance sounds that can also be used to indicate they are in your area. They do not howl like coyotes or wolves, but they do have a loud alarm bark (a slightly drawn-out wail) that can carry half a mile (1 km) or more during calm weather. Once you are familiar with this monosyllabic vocalization, it is not hard to recognize. Sometimes it sounds like a high-pitched bark; other times it can almost be mistaken for the cawing of a crow. But if you listen carefully, you can tell that it is a sound made by an animal with lips and not a beak. It is too high-pitched to be a dog, and too musical to be a crow or a raven. It is often given once or twice per minute in a series of 5 to 15 repetitions. The animal sounds alarmed and excited, and the vocalizations often fade off into the distance as the fox races away. Spring is a good time to listen for this sound, because between April and June, parent foxes often give the alarm bark from various parts of their territory to warn the pups of any dangers.

David Macdonald, Richard Burrows and other British fox researchers talk about the duetting that foxes do between December and February, and they believe it is related to the courtship season. Macdonald describes the sound as a hoarse, strangulated series of shrieks, made by as many as five different foxes spread out over a large area. Sonograms (voice prints) of this call confirm that each fox gives a different pattern. Gunter Tembrock, a German researcher, showed that his tame dog fox responded to his mate's "wow wow wow" vocalization, but not to the same call from other foxes. Macdonald believes that these "contact calls" help foxes locate each other on their territory. I have not heard foxes in my area do this type of duetting, and it seems to be rare in other areas of North America. This difference may represent a behavioral distinction between British and North American red foxes. In any case, the alarm bark and duetting are just two of 40 different sounds that red foxes make, but any of these long-distance vocalizations can help establish whether foxes occupy your area.

Finally, another excellent source of information is your neighbors. Visit with farmers, get involved in local natural history clubs and talk with other amateur naturalists and birders. Let them know you are interested in trying to find red foxes. If there is a local newspaper, write an article or letter asking people to contact you if they have

With small furry ears and a dense coat, the arctic fox is impressively adapted to its polar habitat.

sightings of foxes or know of an active den. This local outreach will increase the number of observers watching for foxes in your area.

What kind of fox is it?

LET'S SAY THAT YOU HAVE identified fox tracks in your area. The next logical question to ask is, what kind of fox is it? To answer this, you need to know the fox species in the Canidae family, and which ones inhabit North America.

"Fox" is not a very accurate scientific term, since a number of different kinds of wild canids are referred to as foxes. The dictionary defines fox as a small wild animal of the Canidae family. Worldwide, there are 21 different fox species. Basically, this group contains three kinds of animals.

Thirteen of the fox species are vulpine foxes, that is, foxes that are members of the *Vulpes* genus, or closely related to that genus. All the North American foxes are vulpine foxes. In South America, there are seven species of foxes of the *Dusicyon* genus. They are small, fox-sized creatures, but are more closely related to the coyote and wolf branch of the dog family. Finally, there is also an African fox species, the bat-eared fox (*Otocyon megalotis*). It is an insect-eating fox that inhabits the African grasslands; up to 70 percent of its diet may consist of termites.

The most common North American species is the red fox (*Vulpes vulpes*). The northernmost fox is the arctic fox (*Alopex lagopus*), an animal that inhabits the tundra not only in North America, but also in Siberia, Russia and across northern Scandinavia. The arctic fox is also found on the coastal regions of Greenland. It is smaller than the red fox, weighing between 3.5 and 8.0 pounds (1.5 to 3.5 kg) and is a slightly more social species than the solitary red fox. In winter, it exhibits two color phases. The most common color is pure white. The other color phase is "blue"— actually a dark to dull slate gray. Blue foxes are more numerous along coastlines and in rocky areas where the ground is not always covered with snow.

Arctic foxes are impressively adapted to

their polar environments. Their winter coat provides such effective insulation that they do not begin to burn extra calories to stay warm until the air temperature has dropped below −22 degrees F (−30 degrees C). Arctic foxes have small, furry ears, and their feet are completely fur-covered. Their eyes have evolved a heavy pigmentation to serve as "snow goggles" to protect against the glare of sun off snow and ice.

When there is a food shortage in the Arctic, such as during the low points of the four-year lemming population cycle, arctic foxes move southward, and a few have shown up in Flin-Flon, Manitoba, and in the northern forests of Saskatchewan and Alberta. During midwinter, arctic foxes typically follow polar bears far out onto the pack ice, trailing after them for long distances hoping to feed on the remains of a seal kill.

In North America, there are two fox species that are highly adapted to arid grasslands and desert environments. These are the swift fox (*Vulpes velox*) and the kit fox (*Vulpes macrotis*). Scientific debate has been going on for decades over whether these two are subspecies of the same species or should be considered different species. Recent research argues that they are both the same species, *Vulpes velox*. The swift and kit foxes are small animals, weighing only 4 to 9 pounds (2 to 4 kg). They have a body length averaging 14 to 18 inches (35 to 45 cm). The kit fox is an animal adapted to the harsh desert environments of the

Weighing only 4 to 9 pounds, swift foxes inhabit the dry grasslands of North America.

Originally a Central American species, the gray fox has extended its range throughout the eastern United States and is found in many parts of the West.

Southwest and has large ears that aid in heat dissipation and in hunting for insects. Interestingly, the kit fox shows a number of adaptations similar to the arctic fox—hair-covered feet, heavily pigmented eyes and an insulating coat of fur. This time the fluffy covering insulates against heat and the cold desert nights, not against the arctic frost. The swift fox inhabits the American prairies and is the most subterranean of our native fox species. It uses dens on its grasslands environment throughout the year and spends most of the daytime hours sleeping near the den or underground.

During prairie wind or snow storms, it seeks the safety of its underground retreats.

The gray fox (*Urocyon cinereoargenteus*) might best be understood as a Central American fox that occupies all regions of Mexico and Central America. However, it also has extended its range throughout the eastern United States, across portions of the American Southwest, and throughout all but the driest regions of California, Nevada and Oregon. The gray fox is slightly smaller than the red fox; it weighs 9 to 11 pounds (4 to 5 kg) and has a head and body length of about 24 inches (60 cm). It has a beautiful salt-and-pepper-colored coat, with a median black stripe on a black-tipped tail. Another name for this fox is the "tree fox" because it can climb trees—albeit not well. Gray foxes, like red foxes, prefer a mixed habitat of fields and woods; however, gray foxes tend to spend more time in the forests, particularly early successional stages of woodlands, while red foxes spend proportionally more of their time along the edge of woodlands and in areas where there is a mix of open areas and woodlots.

If you happen to find a skull, it is usually possible to identify whether it is a wolf, coyote or fox skull. When in the field, examine the skull first by rolling or lifting it with a stick. If there are no maggots or insects, or only a few, then it is perfectly safe to pick up the skull with your hands. Just be sure to keep your hands away from your face until you wash thoroughly.

When you have the skull in your hands, look at the teeth. Were any new molars or other teeth coming in when this animal died? That would indicate that it was a juvenile animal. Look at the sutures (the joints between the head bones). Are they fused in places and is the skull quite solid? These features indicate that the bones of the skull have stopped growing (they grow along the edges of the sutures) and the spots of fused bone indicate you have the skull of an adult canid.

The easiest way to identify if the skull is a wolf, coyote or fox is to measure the total length of the skull along the bottom (ventral) surface. The distance from the front edge of the bone that holds the upper incisors to the back of the bony knobs that rest against the first neck vertebrae is called the condylobasal (cb) length. If the cb length is over 6.5 inches (165 mm), you have found a wolf skull. If the length is between 6.0 and 6.5 inches (150 and 165 mm), you most likely have a coyote skull. If the length is between 4.75 and 6.0 inches (120 and 150 mm), you likely have a gray fox or red fox skull. And between 4.25 and 4.75 inches (105 and 120 mm), you have a swift fox or kit fox skull.

Red foxes and gray foxes coexist over a good portion of North America. How can you distinguish the skulls of these two species? Examine the bony ridges, called temporal ridges, found on the top of the cranium of many mammals. Pick up your fox skull and look down at the top of the cranium from above. The temporal ridges on a red fox skull form a V-shaped pattern, whereas they form a U-shaped pattern on a gray fox skull. V for *Vulpes*; U for *Urocyon*. It's a useful field identification trick.

Measures of the red fox

As you can see from the red fox's vital statistics in the chart on page 30, there is quite a bit of geographic variation within the *Vulpes vulpes* species, with Irish and British red foxes being somewhat larger than the North American subspecies. As I have mentioned, red foxes are the largest vulpine fox, weighing between 9 and 16 pounds (4 and 7 kg) in most areas, with the males being 15 percent larger and heavier than the females. This is only a moderate

Vital Statistics of the Red Fox

~

(Adapted from Macdonald, 1987, and Chapman and Feldhamer, 1982)

Scientific name: *Vulpes vulpes*

Taxonomic family: Canidae

North American dimensions (characterized by wide geographic variation):

    Adult foxes from southern areas: 5.5 to 12.0 pounds (2.5 to 5.5 kg)

    Adult foxes from northern areas: 11.0 to 20.0 pounds (5.0 to 9.0 kg)

    Male-female comparison: males approximately 15 percent heavier

    Total length: 32.5 to 43.1 inches (825 to 1095 mm)

    Tail length: 11.4 to 17.5 inches (290 to 445 mm)

United Kingdom dimensions:

    Adult males: 11.0 to 16.5 pounds (5.0 to 7.5 kg)

    Adult females: 10.0 to 14.5 pounds (4.5 to 6.5 kg)

    Male-female comparison: males approximately 15 percent heavier

    Total length: 33.0 to 49.6 inches (840 to 1260 mm)

    Tail Length: 11.0 to 19.3 inches (280 to 490 mm)

Mating period: January–February (earlier south, later north)

Female estrus: Monestrous, usually 3 days during mating period. On average, 85 percent of young females breed during their first year, but this rate varies widely with social organization and food resources.

Male spermatogenesis: October–February; most young males are capable of breeding during their first year.

Gestation period: 52 to 53 days

Average litter size: 5.2 kits (range: 2 to 7 kits)

Birth weights: 0.16 to 0.26 pounds (71 to 119 grams)

Eyes first open: 8 to 14 days

Weaning: 5 to 8 weeks

Sexual maturity: 9 to 10 months

Adult dental formula: 3/3 incisors, 1/1 canines, 4/4 premolars, 2/3 molars = 42 teeth

Trotting speed: 4 to 8 miles per hour (6 to 13 km per hour)

Maximum speed: 45 miles per hour (72 km per hour)

Average consumption of prey per week:

    Adult foxes: 5.0 pounds (2.25 kg)

    Twelve-week-old kits: 4.2 pounds (1.90 kg)

size difference, and there are no other readily apparent features to distinguish between the sexes. Thus it is often quite a challenge to determine the sex of a free-ranging red fox. Sometimes it is possible to see the penis sheath of a male red fox while he is walking along or urine marking an object. Failing that, your best bet is to study the urine-marking posture that the fox uses. Male red foxes release urine in front of their hind feet (or in front of the tracks of their hind feet in the snow), while female red foxes release urine more from their anal region, so that in snow, the urine marks appear behind the hind feet. Don't be fooled by thinking that male red foxes always lift a leg or that female red foxes always squat—it is much more variable than that. Foxes may use any one of 12 different urine-marking postures, depending on what object they are trying to mark. However, by using the above rule and by seeing the same fox making a urine mark a number of times (or by observing the fox's tracks in relation to the urine mark), it is possible to sex the individual fox reliably. It is just one of the numerous field skills that you will develop.

The danger of rabies

ANYONE WORKING with foxes or other wildlife should be careful about animals infected with rabies.

Rabies is a virus that can infect any warm-blooded animal. Foxes, skunks, raccoons and bats are the main wildlife carriers. Although the disease can be transmitted any time the saliva of an infected animal (or more rarely, its urine, blood or muscle tissue) comes into contact with a small cut or open wound, rabies is usually passed on when an infected animal bites another animal or a person. The rabies virus then infects the nerves and multiplies, growing into the brain, where the infection proliferates. Rabid foxes do not all behave the same. The disease may exhibit itself as "furious" rabies or "dumb" rabies or a combination of the two. In the early stages of furious rabies, the animal changes its disposition: while friendly pets become withdrawn and/or aggressive, a wild fox may become abnormally tame. Animals bite indiscriminately at objects, other animals and people. Normal red foxes avoid porcupines, so stay away from any live or dead red fox with porcupine quills in its mouth. In later stages, the animal becomes excited, runs about aimlessly and gradually develops paralysis in the hind legs and throat (drooling profusely). Eventually it dies. In dumb rabies, the aggressive signs are less noticeable, but the course of the disease is the same.

If you believe you have been exposed to rabies through contact with a wild fox or other animal, flush the wound or exposed area with water immediately. Wash it with soap and water as soon as possible. Remove any clothing that could be contaminated and wash it promptly. Consult your doctor immediately. If the suspected animal can be isolated, do so. But be extremely careful to avoid any contact with the animal. In most areas, you are required by law to report any suspected cases of rabies to the police.

2

The World of the Fox

OXES DON'T SNARL. Wolves do. Dogs do. But not foxes. Why have foxes never evolved this facial expression? They use other displays to communicate threat and aggression. To understand why foxes don't snarl, you have to understand how the world of a fox fits together. This is knowledge that is important for successfully observing foxes.

Wolves and dogs are highly social animals. A wolf is usually a member of a pack, and it depends upon that pack for hunting, for defending its territory and for other basic needs. Red foxes are not pack animals; they are solitary hunters. Snarling is a "close in" facial expression, useful to highly social animals like wolves. It's not of much use to the solitary red fox.

Red foxes, like most organisms, do not exist in a random fashion. They are highly organized individuals, and the way they utilize their space makes great biological sense once you see what type of predator they are and how they make their living.

We'll piece together our puzzle of the fox's life by focusing on two field signs created by red foxes: dens and scats. Even if the foxes in your area are secretive and elusive animals, you are likely to encounter these two signs in your field work. They are immensely valuable sources of information if you know how to use them.

After exploring dens and scats, we'll survey what researchers have found out about how red foxes organize their living space.

A mother fox typically picks a hillside with easy-to-dig sandy or loamy soil as a den site, *above.* Usually a source of water is nearby. *Opposite:* a kit in the forest near its den.

Then we'll examine some of the major social events on the fox's yearly calendar and take a close look at how adult foxes raise their young. With this information, you will be much better equipped to search for and observe wild red foxes.

Finding a den

How DO YOU FIND an active fox den and where should you search for it? At the outset, it is important to know that a family of foxes on its territory will have not one but numerous dens tucked here and there, and these lairs will be used for different purposes at different times of the year. The foxes that I have studied often have a dozen or more very simple dens that they retreat to in times of bad weather or danger. These dens typically have a single entrance dug into a hillside with a 6-to-10-foot tunnel

A six-week-old kit, sporting its telltale sandy coat, peers out of the entrance of its den.

that opens into a small chamber where the fox curls up and sleeps until the storm has abated or the danger has passed. Periods of heavy rain, strong winds or fierce snowstorms, as well as the presence of hunters or predators in the area, will cause foxes to escape underground into these types of dens. Biologists refer to them as shelter dens or sleeping dens, and both sexes, adult and young, use them during adverse or dangerous times.

The most highly developed dens on the fox's home range are the natal dens, the dens in which the pups are born and raised. The parent foxes may have several well-developed natal dens upon their territory, and each year the vixen will choose one of them for her pups.

The natal den of a red fox is frequently an abandoned groundhog burrow, an old badger hole or a den previously used by a red fox that has lain abandoned for several years. The vixen chooses one and, over time, excavates additional entrances, tunnels and chambers until the den is fully developed for her kits.

Some vixens can be quite foxy in their efforts to keep the natal den looking abandoned during the first month of the kits' life, which is spent mostly underground. During this time, some vixens restrict their comings and goings to one burrow and reduce the number of tracks that they leave around the den. Numerous times I have judged a den inactive only to find out later that there were young fox kits hidden inside it. Through these types of disappointing experiences, I have devised several systems for determining whether a den is occupied.

One of the best ways to tell if an animal the size of an adult fox is entering and leaving the den is to look for spider webs or single strands of a spider's silk across the tunnel entrance you are investigating. It has been my experience that if a fox-sized animal has not gone in and out of the den for two weeks, these strands begin to appear.

I have often set a blade of grass or created a cross out of two blades of grass in the entrances of a suspected fox den and then checked one or two days later to see if they have been disturbed, indicating that an animal has entered or left the tunnel during that time. I have found this technique extremely helpful when searching for active dens.

By measuring the average diameter of the tunnel, I can identify whether a den belongs to a wolf, coyote or red fox. This is an easy field procedure. With a tape measure, get down on your stomach and reach into each of the tunnels of a den as far as you can. Measure the diameter of the tunnels until you have 20 or 30 different measurements for that den. Then figure out the average of these measurements. The natal dens of wolves usually have tunnels with an average diameter of 20

The vixen will often select an abandoned groundhog burrow, an old badger hole or a den once used by another fox. To determine if a den is unoccupied, check for spider webs across the tunnel entrance.

inches (50 cm) or more. They are big enough for a person to crawl or squirm into. In fact, the hardest thing to decide about a den of this size is whether it is a wolf den or a den used by a hibernating black bear.

When juvenile red foxes first leave their dens, they often travel in pairs or as threes.

Both animals dig tunnels of approximately the same diameter. If the den has multiple entrances, it is probably a wolf natal den. If the den has only a single entrance leading into a fairly large, roundish chamber with branches and other bedding material in it, then it is more likely used by a hibernating black bear. Also, for all dens, look for strands of hair caught on roots or in surrounding shrubs. They may help identify what animal has used the den. Hair from a black bear is long, wiry and is a single color. Hair from a wolf is short, straight and is often silver-tipped. (By examining the hair under a microscope, you can see patterns of scales on the hair. There are guidebooks available for identifying most species of mammals from the pattern of the scales on a single strand of hair.)

In my study area, the dens of coyotes have tunnels that, on average, measure 15 inches in diameter, give or take about 2 inches (38 cm ± 5 cm). Red foxes dig tunnels that measure on average 10 inches, give or take 2 inches (25 cm ± 5 cm). So in addition to tracks and scats, the diameters of the tunnels can be very helpful in identifying which species has dug the den.

There is good reason behind this pattern. Given the chance, wolves have been observed to kill adult and young coyotes, and coyotes have been observed to kill adult and young foxes. Wolves at times seem tolerant of red foxes, while at other times, wolves readily kill them. Although there is variation in the interactions between wolves and foxes, the consistent pattern is: wolves kill coyotes, coyotes kill foxes. Thus I believe there has been strong selection pressure among these wild canids to dig dens that exclude larger species. Coyotes dig tunnels that are not large enough to accommodate adult wolves, and red foxes dig tunnels that are not large enough to accommodate adult coyotes.

When a vixen is selecting a site for her natal den, what features does she seem to look for? After carefully observing 65 dens in my area, I find that red fox natal dens often show the following characteristics: They are usually in the forest, but close to a meadow or open slope, and they often have multiple entrances. The natal den is also normally within 100 yards (90 m) of a water source, although this can be as small as a standing pool or as large as a vast northern lake. The usefulness of some of these features, such as the closeness of drinking water, is obvious, but some of the others need explanation. The open area provides a space where the vixen can sun and where the rambunctious pups can play freely. In addition, the vixen often chooses a burrow previously made by a groundhog, skunk, fox or other animal, and one where the den is located on a hillside in sandy, loamy soil. The fact that vixens almost always dig the natal den in sandy, loamy soil turned into a fox evolution puzzle that took me several years to understand.

Vixens probably select such soil because they can dig into it easily. As I mentioned in the first chapter, fox claws are more slender and sharper that the claws of other canid species. Sharp claws assist the fox in its hunting behavior and are used for pinning small prey to the ground. The trade-off is that the red fox is not as efficient a digger as a dog, coyote or wolf. For these reasons, the red fox often takes over dens abandoned by other animals and prefers to dig in soft soil.

There are other ecological pressures guiding the vixen to select sandy-colored soil for the natal den. When they are born,

In the early spring, the female fox gives birth to between 3 and 6 kits. Different color phases can occur within the same litter.

fox kits are not the bright red color of adult foxes. Like many other carnivore species, they have a special natal coat—in the case of red fox kits, they are charcoal gray, often with a white tip at the end of the tail. I believe that this special natal coat is an infantile characteristic that helps to endear the young to the parents and helps establish a strong bond between them.

However, at about five weeks of age, when the kits begin to spend increasingly large amounts of time above ground, an important change in their coat takes place. This juvenile coat is not the brilliant red fur of an adult fox, but sandy-colored fur that matches the soil of the den site to an impressive degree. This helps camouflage the kits around the den site and protects them from occasional predators, such as hawks, owls and coyotes.

I believe that the juvenile pelage evolved like this: At first vixens tended to dig their natal dens in sandy soil simply because it afforded good digging, but over time, the fur of the kits slowly evolved to match the sandy color of the soil. That is, if sandy-colored pups had even a slightly better chance of surviving over time, fox kits would tend to evolve this adaptive coloration. When this happened, it created a greater selection pressure for the vixens to locate their dens in sandy-colored soil. The selection of the den by the vixen and the juvenile pelage of the kits are features that

At about five weeks, a kit fox's coat turns sandy-colored, camouflaging it from predators.

biologists call "coadapted" characteristics. They help protect the young during their vulnerable first month outside the den.

Vixens protect their pups in other ways as well. Dick Decker, a fox biologist from Edmonton, Alberta, discovered an interesting pattern between foxes and coyotes in the farmlands of central Alberta. Farmers in this area usually enjoy having foxes around, but they strongly dislike coyotes. Decker found that red foxes prefer to den adjacent to roads, near granaries or close to farm buildings, and he suggests that these are the areas that coyotes tend to avoid because of the risk of being shot at by farmers. The roads and farm buildings have thus created a belt of coyote-free lands in which the foxes raise their young and do most of their traveling and hunting. Dennis Voigt, a researcher from Ontario, has also shown that red foxes generally do not frequent an area inhabited by coyotes. Generally, the two species divide up the countryside.

A scat by any other name

IN THE FIRST CHAPTER, we discovered how a field biologist identifies a scat as one from a red fox, and the safety precautions that must be followed in collecting and studying droppings. Their main use is to determine the food habits of the species from the remains that are excreted in the scat. Bits of leaves, small bones, single strands of hair and seeds can all be used to determine what the foxes have eaten.

I started my research on foxes by reviewing 158 different studies of the red fox's food habits, carried out in many different parts of the world. These studies highlight

On average, fox droppings measure 2.5 inches long. They should never be handled.

two important facts about their diet: First, it is best described as catholic—the red fox eats a wide variety of foods, and its diet changes from season to season. Second, the fox is an opportunistic feeder who will sample any acceptable food, often in proportion to its availability. A study done in Missouri is typical. It found that foxes in that area had eaten 34 different mammals, 14 species of birds, 15 families of insects and 21 species of plants. However, most animals and plant species contributed less than 1 percent by volume to the bulk of the fox's diet. While red foxes sample many different foods, they tend to rely on a small number

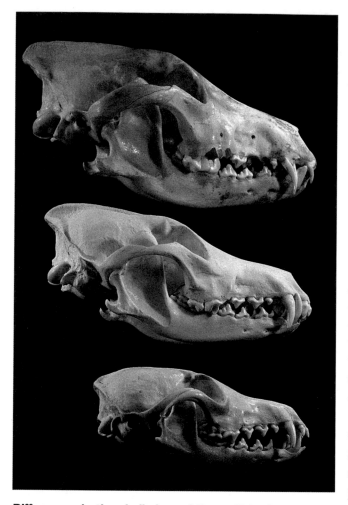

Differences in the skull sizes of the wolf *(top)*, coyote *(middle)*, and fox *(bottom)* reflect the size of their prey.

fruit and berries. The upper size limit of prey that will be hunted by a red fox is no larger than a jackrabbit. Understanding which foods are the staples of the fox's diet in your area and where these foods are abundant can be a great help to you in locating red foxes.

Notice that birds are not in this list of staples. The only time red foxes have been found to be efficient predators of birds is during the spring when certain species of ducks, grouse and gulls nest on the ground. Red foxes sometimes have quite an impact on ground-nesting birds and their eggs. However, during the rest of the year, foxes do not seem to be able to catch birds effectively.

The red fox is not a scaled-down wolf. It is an entirely different type of predator—a solitary hunter. Wolves hunt in packs, and they hunt deer, elk and moose—prey considerably larger than a single wolf. The members of the pack cooperate in capturing and killing these large-bodied prey. Foxes hunt small prey, animals that a single fox can readily kill. Killing is the easy part for a fox; catching these alert small animals that quickly flee down a burrow or up a tree is the major challenge. To do so, the fox uses a stealthy, catlike form of hunting. When the fox is successful, it ends up with a mouse-sized meal, only large enough to

as their staples. The Missouri study found that three items—the cottontail rabbit, the meadow vole and insects—comprised more than 60 percent of the foxes' nourishment. Red foxes take advantage of seasonably abundant food, but over the course of a year, they seem to rely on a limited number of plant and animal species. These usually include small rodents, rabbits, insects, wild

feed a single fox.

Once you understand this much about the fox's hunting behavior, its activity patterns also begin to make sense. Red foxes are usually crepuscular, that is, active at night but most active around dusk and dawn. Keep this in mind when you are planning your fox-watching excursions. Why are foxes most on the move then? These are the times when their small prey are most active. The fox's activity patterns mirror those of its quarry. During winter, when mice and voles become more active during daylight hours because they live in a twilight world under the snow, I find that red foxes become more active during the daytime as well.

Knowing the fox's hunting behavior can also provide an understanding of what constitutes prime habitat for the species. Populations of red foxes do best, that is, they become most abundant, in country that is varied—land that is made up of a patchwork of woodlot, open meadows, dense brushland, pastures and small wetlands. The more diverse an area is, the more red foxes seem to thrive in it. Ernest Thompson Seton once described red foxes as "animals of half-open country."

Biologists who have radio-tracked foxes for long periods find that they spend a great deal of their time traveling along ecotones, the scientific term for the edge where two habitats meet — for example, where woods and meadows join. One of the best places to watch for foxes is in these areas. These edge environments often exhibit the densest and most diverse vegetation because plants from both habitats grow there. Amid this lush vegetation, small rodents, rabbits, birds and insects often find better food, shelter and nesting spots. Because of this abundant prey, red foxes are often observed to be "predators of the edge."

Fox society

FOXES TRAVEL ALONE. When you observe foxes, you will mostly be watching solitary animals. However, this does not mean that the solitary fox is not aware of and does not communicate with the foxes that live around it. Most researchers have found that red foxes exist on family territories. A territory is a particular piece of space actively defended by an animal against other members of the same species.

A seven-week old kit begs food from its mother, who has just returned to the den from hunting.

While family territories appear to be the basic social unit of red fox populations, there is interesting variation to the pattern. Environmental factors influence the size of the territory. In the rich farmlands around Oxford, England, David Macdonald and his colleagues have found fox families that have a territory as small as 10 hectares, roughly 24 acres. Even though the foxes could run across the entire length of the territory in a minute or two, they stay within its confines, with only the occasional trip beyond the borders. What environmental conditions hold them on such small territories? Macdonald found that food is always abundant on these territories; the fox population of the area is dense, and there appears to be no compelling reason for the foxes to defend a larger area. On the other hand, studying foxes in southeastern Iran, David Macdonald has found that in the impoverished desert environment, a fox family territory measures approximately 5,000 hectares (12,000 acres) in size. Oman fox territories are 500 times larger than Oxford territories. This variation shows how adaptive red foxes can be to different conditions.

In the high Arctic and in the cultivated prairie regions of the American West, fox family territories tend to be between 3,000 and 4,000 hectares (7,500 to 10,000 acres). Both of these environments are characterized by sparse or fluctuating small-mammal populations. In the rich farmlands of southern Sweden, Torbjorn von Schantz found

Juvenile foxes hunt together. When mature, foxes seldom travel with each other.

that red fox territories average about 400 hectares (1,000 acres), while in the Swedish taiga where food is more scarce, Eric Lindstrom found the red fox family territories to be up to 1,200 hectares (3,000 acres) in size.

It should also be kept in mind that some foxes will be found that are not living on a family territory. Juvenile foxes that are dispersing or foxes that face a food collapse on their territory will move through a considerable area searching for a vacant territory with adequate food resources.

The family plot

RED FOXES ARE USUALLY observed traveling alone. Yet families of foxes seem to be the basic social group around which red fox populations are organized. Are red foxes solitary or social? Well, it depends on how one uses these terms. Red foxes seldom travel together and never operate as a pack. Courtship and breeding are the only times of year when adult foxes are seen together. To my mind, this makes the red fox a solitary species.

But recent research has repeatedly shown that the social life of solitary animals is much richer than we have previously understood. To be solitary does not mean the animal does not have a social life; it means that its social interactions are often different from those of highly social species. For instance, an animal like the red fox, traveling by itself on its territory, stays in touch with other members of its family through urine marks and other types of scent marking. Long-distance vocalizations inform other members of the fox family where a mate and offspring are operating on the family territory. Red foxes do not howl as the highly social wolf and moderately social coyote do; but red foxes do give loud, sharp alarm barks. Listen for these barks.

Foxes of different territories also communicate through territorial scent markings. These territorial boundaries may be extremely crisply defined in key foraging

As kits become older, they turn almost puppylike and can be observed engaging in social play.

areas or in prime hunting habitat, while territorial owners may tolerate a good deal of overlap and neighborly intrusion in the less important and less productive regions of their territory.

What groups of foxes are you likely to find on one of these territories, that is, what does a fox family look like? Again, we see considerable variation that correlates well with food conditions, the density of foxes in the area and other factors. In the food-rich area of southern England, the fox families on a territory tend to average four to six adult foxes. Usually, only one of the adults is a male, and the others tend to be a vixen with several of her young (but fully grown) female offspring. When these foxes make up a family, there is usually a strong dominance hierarchy among the females, and only the older, dominant vixen breeds and gives birth to pups. The younger, subordinate vixens are called "helpers" because they bring food to the pups, play with them and help to raise them in other ways. Several researchers have even seen helper females nurse the kits of a dominant vixen. In Macdonald's area, these families have been stable for a number of years. In other areas, the helper females remain on their parents' territory for a year or two, and then disperse, pairing up with a young male fox on newly established territory, where they can breed and raises kits of their own.

Obviously, then, there is considerable variation in what constitutes a fox family. It may consist of a single dog fox and a single vixen raising a litter of pups. Or it may consist of one dominant dog fox and up to five vixens, all of whom cooperate in raising a single litter of kits—or any condition in between.

What determines the form that a specific fox family adopts? Evolutionary theory tells us that, within a species, animals that are

While still living in the den, the pups begin to eat wild berries and hunt for insects.

best adapted to their environment survive better and leave more offspring than other animals in that population. Genetically inherited characteristics that enable an animal to adapt to its environment and thus help it to leave more offspring become more common in the population as generations go by. This is how evolution works, and the yardstick of success is the number of surviving offspring that an individual leaves.

In my northern study area (as compared to Macdonald's study area in productive British farmlands), food resources vary greatly from year to year as snowshoe hares and small rodents build up and then die off in dramatic population cycles. In northern Saskatchewan, fox density is low, and foxes must coexist with coyotes and wolves. Here,

fox families normally consist of one dog fox and one vixen raising a litter of pups. However, about a third of the fox families also have helper vixens, usually one and only rarely two helpers per family.

But when the snowshoe hares are at the peak of their population cycle, food resources become truly abundant, and during these years a dog fox may breed two vixens, and two litters of pups are raised on his territory. Normally, the vixens give birth to their litters in separate natal dens, and the dog fox brings food to both vixens. As the pups get older, the vixens spend more of their time hunting for food on the family territory. Instead of competing, the vixens are highly tolerant of each other. This suggests that the vixens are familiar with each other and are probably related. In fact, in several cases I have observed the vixens move their pups, once the kits are a month or more of age, to a common den and raise them together. Since the vixens may give birth to their pups up to a month apart, this arrangement explains how a den may contain pups that are clearly at different stages of development. It all makes sense if it is understood as a fox family's way of making use of abundant food resources occurring on the territory that spring.

Why do some vixens become helper vixens, expending energy in helping to raise the dominant vixen's kits instead of searching for a vacant territory and raising a litter of their own? The answer lies in an evolutionary force that bears down on any species of animal: kin selection. As theoretical biologist W.D. Hamilton explained, kin selection means that individual animals have a vested interest not just in the survival of their own offspring, but also in that of other blood relatives. This is because brothers, sisters and cousins also share common genes. By helping these genes survive into the next generation, a helper fox is maximizing the survival of its own genes. So a helper vixen acting as a nanny can improve the survival of her kin. Under certain food and environmental conditions (high fox density, stable food resources), a helper vixen may make a greater contribution to the next generation by staying on her parents' territory and helping her younger brothers and sisters to survive. Perhaps she will eventually inherit the territory of her mother. In any case, staying home and

helping is a better bet than setting off on her own where her chances of surviving and finding a vacant territory are extremely low. It is the balancing of such factors that determines the forms that fox families take.

Observing at a den

ANY ACTIVE DEN where adult red foxes are raising their kits affords a wonderful opportunity to study these animals on a day-to-day basis. But be careful. You will want to proceed with caution for good reasons: certainly you will not want to do anything that could endanger the welfare of the kits, and if you do anything that alarms or irritates the adult foxes, they will move the pups to a new, more secretive den, and your study will vanish before your eyes.

Let's say that you have discovered an active fox natal den where a dog fox and vixen are raising a litter of young pups. Things are at the stage where the pups are just beginning to come above ground; the kits are mostly charcoal gray with the sandy-colored juvenile coat just beginning to appear on the head and shoulders. This pelage condition would tell you that the pups are four or, at most, five weeks of age. A quiet, attentive observer will see that the dog fox and vixen are making regular trips to the den, particularly in the morning and evening. When the vixen arrives, she usually nurses the pups, but the kits are also beginning to eat small prey brought in by the dog fox and vixen. How should you go about studying this family of red foxes?

You stand on the threshold of one of the

At about five weeks of age, the pups increase their play with siblings and parents.

most interesting chapters to be found in the life of a red fox. But you'll benefit by some hard-earned advice about how to proceed. There are many questions. Should you use a blind? Should you dress in camouflage clothing? How far should you locate yourself from the den?

The most important point to realize is that it is the foxes' choice whether they will allow you to study them or not. You are hanging by a very delicate thread. Let me repeat: if you do anything that even slightly annoys or frightens the adult foxes, one of them—usually the vixen—will move the pups to a new den. On several occasions, I have searched 10 hours a day for more than a week trying to relocate a litter of pups af-

ter a vixen has moved them and have never found the new den site.

There is no way you can hide yourself from the hypersensitive nose of a red fox. The parents will know that you are there. Some researchers claim to have luck with blinds and camouflage clothing, but I think the most important thing to keep in mind is for you to act in a polite, considerate manner and avoid at all costs disturbing the pups or alarming the adults. In your movements walking to or watching from your observation spot, be relaxed or quiet, not tense, excited or nervous. Don't arrive at the den during dusk or dawn when the foxes are most active. Regardless of whatever ridiculous or inconvenient hour is involved, go

In early summer, the kits spend hours waiting for their parents to return with food.

to the den and leave the den during times when the pups are underground sleeping and the adults are not in the area. Begin observing at a safe distance—several hundred yards if possible—and only slowly move in closer. There is an invisible boundary around the den that varies with each parent fox. I cannot tell you where it is—some foxes will tolerate you at a distance of 20 feet (6 m), and other foxes will not tolerate you at 100 yards (90 m). But if the parent fox finds you within that boundary once, the pups will be moved to a new location that same night. However, if you conduct yourself wisely, you may be able to observe

red foxes at one of the most important and interesting times in their lives.

In my northern study area, the kits are born during late March or early April. In more southern areas, they can be born more than a month and a half earlier. When they are born, the kits normally number between three and six and usually weigh less than a quarter of a pound (100 g) each. Fox kits grow slowly during the first few weeks, and their eyes do not open until they are 10 or 12 days old. In southern areas, the vixen may leave the den after two days, but in northern areas, she stays constantly in the den from a few days before birth until the kits are approximately 10 days old. She is completely dependent on the dog fox for food during this time. David Macdonald suggests that the kits are so small and vulnerable during early life that the vixen must surround them with her warm body if they are to survive. The vixen may be preheating the den before the pups are born, and then she virtually forms a thermal blanket, protecting the kits in their frosty underground chamber.

When the cubs are approximately two weeks old, the vixen begins spending more and more time away from the den hunting prey for herself, but she does return at regular intervals to nurse the pups. While she is there, she plays and naps with them and grooms them, cleaning out their ears, licking their groins and eating their waste products. She continues these activities until the pups are about five weeks old and ready to be weaned.

The early life of a fox kit is not as carefree as one might imagine. At about 25 days of age, while the kits are still spending most of their time underground, they begin to fight viciously and clash with each other in short, serious and, in rare cases, fatal contests. If you listen closely, you can hear these fights taking place underground. Sometimes they break out above ground as well. The fox kits scrap on and off over the next 10 days or so and, in the process, establish a strict dominance hierarchy. The alpha, or dominant, cub establishes itself, and the hierarchy continues all the way down to the omega, or most submissive, animal. This hierarchy determines the access that each pup has to the food brought by the parents and dictates who can steal food from whom. If the parents are bringing in only a limited amount of prey (because prey is scarce on the family territory), the dominant pups get a larger proportion of the food and have the best chance of surviving, while the smaller and submissive ones may perish. The runt of the litter dies first, then the second lowest on the hierarchy and so on. It is a brutal process, but one that adjusts the size of the litter to food resources and maximizes the chances for the greatest number of pups to survive.

When the pups are four or five weeks old, they begin to come above ground for longer periods, and this is the time when the prime observing opportunities begin. At this point, the hierarchy is solidly established and aggressiveness between the

During early life, fox kits fight viciously until they have established a strict dominance order.

kits decreases and disappears. They become more social, playful and puppylike. Over the next several weeks, the kits interact with one another and with their parents, and a naturalist can observe hunting, fighting and food-caching behaviors developing. The foxes seem genetically programmed to try out these motor patterns in sessions of play fighting and play hunting, and it is fascinating to watch young foxes practicing and perfecting these adult behaviors.

During these weeks, an observer can watch the parent foxes continue to hunt and scavenge at different times of the day and night to supply the kits with food. The adult foxes bring in a veritable parade of prey and present it to the pups. It may be that the parents are trying to expose the kits to the widest variety of food sources available on the family territory. In one week, I have seen one family of kits' menu include mice, voles, hares, squirrels, groundhogs, songbirds, grouse and a spawning long-nose sucker.

Food is distributed at the den in a vulpine ritual that is always the same. Carrying the food in its mouth, the adult fox arrives at the den, chortles a "wuk-wuk-wuk," and one or more of the pups rushes out. The first pup to approach the parent crouches low and beats its tail around wildly, whining and creeping toward the adult. Then, reaching up, it smells, licks and bites at the corner of the adult's mouth.

Young foxes hone adult skills through sessions of mock hunting (above) and mock fighting.

The adult gives the food to the first pup that begs for it. This seems to be the mechanism by which the food is more or less evenly distributed; however, once the pup has its food, its real problems begin. It now has to defend its prize against its litter mates. The kit tries to do this by running off or by threatening any sibling who comes near. Often, a dominant kit will challenge and steal the provision from one of its subordinate litter mates.

This food-begging behavior appears later in a fox's life but in a completely different context—as a submissive display between adults. When two full-grown foxes meet, the subordinate fox often acts as if it is a young fox begging to be fed.

Gradually, kits become more confident outside the den and venture further afield each day.

It crouches low, whines, and beats its tail madly in every direction. This keeps the white tip of the tail in constant motion (much like waving a white handkerchief), letting the tail function as an attention-getting device. The subordinate fox slowly creeps up to the dominant fox and carefully reaches up and smells and licks the corner of the dominant's mouth. The formerly puppylike behavior has evolved to become one of the main submissive displays used by adult foxes.

During June, the pups spend endless hours playing, interacting and waiting for the adults to arrive with food. But as the pups get older, the adults spend more and more time away from the den. When an adult appears, one pup gets the food, which he quickly consumes, then the adult frequently takes one or several pups on exploratory trips away from the den site. At first, the parents lead the kits away and return with them. Later, the kits return on their own. What takes place on these sorties away from the den is one of the areas of fox behavior that no one yet has been able to study.

The kits, while hanging around the den, begin to eat wild strawberries and hunt for insects and whatever prey they can find in the immediate area. Gradually, they become more confident and venture farther afield each day, spending less time at the den. It seems that through a combination of boredom and hunger, the parent foxes eventually drive the kits away from the den

It may look vicious, but it's all in good fun as these kits engage in a session of play fighting.

site to begin a predatory, scavenging life of their own. At first, the pups travel in groups of two or three, but because their prey are small and quick and must be hunted in a catlike manner, the young foxes soon learn to become solitary predators.

For the remainder of the summer, the kits hunt and make a living on the family territory. During this time, when the vixen and pups rendezvous, they often greet, play and generally enjoy each other, but by this point the dog fox is intolerant of his off-

spring and shows mild aggressive behavior when they approach.

No one is certain what finally causes the kits to leave the territory. Adult foxes have not been seen to drive their young away, but they may exclude them from the best hunting and scavenging areas. Whatever the cause, during late September or October, the kits begin to disperse. Males leave first and travel the farthest. Young male foxes often journey long distances, more or less in a straight line, in search of a vacant territory. The record for a dispersing male fox is more than 300 miles (500 km), recorded in Sweden.

Dispersal is a time of high vulnerability and risk for these young foxes. If they enter the occupied territory of another fox, they are viciously attacked by the territorial owners—usually the dominant dog fox or dominant vixen. Typically, as soon as the dog fox sees the other fox, he charges and attacks it without giving any warning displays. The young fox turns and runs, and a fast chase ensues. If the territory owner catches the intruder, there is much "gekkering" (a deep-throated, raspy sound), and the two foxes tumble around on the ground, slamming hips into each other and viciously biting at the face and paws or whatever body parts of the opponent come within reach. Usually, the intruding fox flees, and if caught again, there is more tumbling and fighting. The fight terminates when the intruding fox leaves the territory of the dominant fox, and after this experience, the young fox rarely returns for more. Dominant vixens have been observed to attack young dispersing female foxes in a similar manner, and some attacks across sexes have also been documented. This is fox aggression at its most intense.

Aggression between parent and offspring or between neighboring foxes is much less intense and more ritualized. Threat displays include arching the back while erecting the body hair to make the fox look as large as possible. Another threat display consists of two foxes rising up and pressing their forepaws against each other's shoulders while jaw-gaping and gekkering. In low-intensity aggressive encounters, the dominant fox walks stiff-legged and stares at the subordinate fox who crouches down and thrashes its tail back and forth while begging puppylike at the corner of the dominant fox's mouth.

Eventually, a young male and young female fox find each other on a vacant territory and a pair bond forms. This is how a new fox family comes to be. In my area, during late December or early January, courtship begins. It is not difficult to tell when the courtship season for red foxes has commenced. As I have mentioned, the urine marks of red foxes take on a much stronger odor at that time. Furthermore, fox tracks suddenly become paired. Both signs are clear indications that courtship has begun.

For approximately two weeks, fox tracks stay paired with the male usually traveling after and attending the female. The female fox normally has only a single estrous period per year that lasts several days. Once breeding has taken place, the pair resume their solitary traveling and hunting on the family territory. After a gestation period of approximately 52 days, the vixen is ready to give birth. Typically, during the last week or two of the gestation period, she spends a good deal of time sleeping near the natal den and retreats underground several days before birth takes place, and the cycle of the fox's life begins again.

3

Appearance Counts

IN THE RED FOX, beauty and adaptation become one—its most elegant features are also some of its most important tools for survival. For instance, the long tapering limbs, gazellelike body and yellow serpentine eyes of the fox are stunning characteristics, but they are also physical features that help make the animal an effective hunter. But it is not easy to understand the beauty of the fox. Consider its improbable pumpkin-colored coat, black velvety ears and magnificent brush of a tail. Why does the red fox flaunt such conspicuous features when most predators prudently emphasize camouflage?

In this chapter, we will try to look at the red fox as if it were a work of art, a masterpiece of nature. But in this circumstance, the sculptor is evolution, and the interpretation is ecological. Why has *Vulpes vulpes* evolved certain features, and how do these features help red foxes adapt?

The survival value of some features—

sharp teeth, for instance—is obvious. Detailed research is necessary to understand the adaptive functions of other features, and I will try to summarize what is known about them. The adaptive value of still other vulpine features remains a mystery waiting for future field biologists to decipher. Many characteristics have multiple functions and contexts. Discovering new reasons and new adaptive uses behind the appearance of the red fox is an ongoing process filled with surprises.

Let's start with the fox's coat. The first thing to understand is that not all red foxes are bright orange. Red foxes inherit different coat colors, just as humans inherit different colors of hair. Furthermore, the common red color becomes less frequent, and other coat colors more common, the farther north one goes. Red, cross and black are the three main color phases of *Vulpes vulpes*. However, foxes within each of these color phases vary considerably. For example, the normal red coat varies from a light amber color to a dark red. Some black foxes stay black during the whole year, while others turn silver during the winter

---

While other predators appear camouflaged, a red fox flaunts a red coat, black ears and a magnificent white-tipped tail.

Arctic foxes exhibit two color phases, white, _(left)_ and blue, depending on the habitat.

when their silver-tipped guard hairs grow up through their black summer coat. Black and silver foxes are relatively rare in southern regions but are frequently encountered in the northern forest or on the Arctic tundra.

There are other genetically determined coat colors of _Vulpes vulpes_. The so-called "bastard" fox has a bluish gray appearance, and "Samson" foxes exhibit no guard hairs, so that only the curly underwool is present in their coat. It's important to realize that all these differently colored foxes are indeed the same species. These variations in coat color do not exist to the same extent in other fox species; it is a feature most highly developed in _Vulpes vulpes_. The arctic fox shows two color phases, white and blue, and its coat color is usually correlated with whether the winter habitat of a particular fox is snow-covered or not. Swift foxes, kit foxes and gray foxes certainly show some limited variation in coat color, but not the prominently different color phases.

Several researchers have observed that black foxes, and to a lesser extent cross foxes, seem to be more placid and less aggressive than lightly colored red and amber foxes. R.D. Guthrie, a researcher from Alaska, has suggested that the darker foxes may be at an advantage when fox populations are abundant, and lighter colored foxes may be at an advantage when fox densities are low. However, the field testing of this hypothesis has given unclear results. To date, we do not understand why _Vulpes vulpes_ has evolved such distinctly different coat colors.

Fox tails

ONE OF THE MOST intriguing characteristics of the red fox—indeed to many people its hallmark—is its magnificent tail. The tail is approximately two-thirds as long as the rest of the fox, and during winter, when the tail is at its fluffiest, it sometimes looks like a cloud traveling along, attached to this speedy predator.

For years, naturalists have referred to the tail as the "brush." The distinctive white tip at the end of the tail is called the "tag" and is one of the best field signs for identifying red foxes. The tag is present even in newborn pups, and red foxes are the only species of canid in North America that regularly shows this identifying white marking.

Why does the red fox have a white-tipped tail? After a great deal of observing, I've come up with this hypothesis about its adaptive uses: Over much of its geographical range, red foxes frequent densely vegetated environments and are often active in the reduced-light conditions of dusk, dawn and night. In short, they live in environments where visibility is restricted. My field observations show that when one fox wishes to greet and identify itself to another fox as well as demonstrate its submissiveness, it crouches close to the ground and lashes its tail back and forth excitedly. I think the white tag of the tail combined with tail lashing has evolved as an attention-getting display that is effective even under reduced visibility. Furthermore, red foxes are very much like domestic cats in the way their attention can be mesmerized by a small moving object. The white tag on the tail could also function to fixate the attention of the dominant fox on the moving tag and away from the submissive animal.

The fox's brush can communicate in other ways. On the upper surface of the tail, about a third of the way down its length, there is a patch of dark fur. Under this dark patch, there is a well-developed scent gland called the subcaudal gland. When members

With its white tip, the tail of a fox acts as a communication aid in dense underbrush.

To reduce heat loss, foxes sleep with their tails curled around their nose and paws.

their legs, paws and nose to reduce heat loss. The foxes I have studied literally sleep on their tails during the summertime and sleep under their tails during the coldest parts of winter.

Ear and tail communication

WHEN YOU WATCH two foxes interact, notice how they communicate through ear and tail signals, much like other members of the dog family. An erect tail sloping up at a steep angle combined with ears flattened on the neck are display signals of a confident fox ready to attack another fox. The fox's tail wrapped closely along its side or between its legs combined with flattened ears and a crouched posture indicate a highly submissive fox. A tail that forms an upside-down U, combined with ears held flattened but sticking out from the side of the head, are signs of play. These tail and ear postures grade into one another and produce an array of communicative displays—perplexing to human observers but readily decipherable by foxes.

of a fox family meet, they often sniff one another's subcaudal gland as part of their greeting ritual. The dark patch of fur over the gland may be a target for the other fox to sniff at, and it may help to disseminate the odor of the gland as the fur is warmed by the rays of the sun.

The brush of the red fox has other characteristics that appear to have survival value. The tail has tremendous loft; that is, its fluffiness gives it considerable insulating value. During cold periods, I have observed sleeping foxes with their tails curled around

Another feature that relates to fox communication is the coloration of the ears. The velvety black surfaces of the backs of the ears combined with the buff-colored fronts and dark interiors create a unique color code for each major ear posture with which red foxes communicate. Under reduced light or in dense vegetation, even when the ear posture of the signaling fox cannot be seen by the other fox, the receiving fox can make out the color code of the ear signal. I believe it works somewhat like a semaphore system: instead of using two flags and various arm positions, the fox uses ear positions, but each position also has a unique color code.

A subtle adaptation shown by red foxes is the buff-colored spots on their shoulders. These cream-colored shoulder spots are usually present in all the color phases of *Vulpes vulpes*. Their subdued appearance belies their important function. They are used largely as targets—ritualized aggression is often directed at these shoulder spots. Ritualized aggression occurs not during the free-for-all fights between a territory owner and unknown intruder, but in more inhibited contests, such as a skirmish between neighboring foxes on a territorial boundary or between a parent fox and its offspring. During ritualized aggression, the bites of the attacking fox are frequently di-

rected at the other fox's shoulder spots. Sometimes an attacking fox will lunge into the air and come down from above, opening its mouth wide enough to bite at both of these shoulder targets. Not only are the scapulae bones fairly well equipped to absorb bites, but the skin on this region of the fox's body is reinforced with collagen fibers to absorb these attacks. A dominance struggle between these foxes is often settled through this type of ritualized aggression without either fox being seriously injured.

There are many features of the fox's external appearance that biologists still do not understand. The dark spot on the fox's muzzle or the white facial markings and white chest markings that some red foxes show—these features remain mysteries. Do these markings have a communication function? How do these features help a fox

Like dogs, red foxes use ear, body and tail postures as important communication displays.

to survive and prosper? There is still much to learn about why red foxes are built the way they are.

The catlike canid

THERE IS NO DOUBT that the red fox is a member of the dog family, Canidae. It shows many of the typical characteristics of this taxonomic group. The skull and skeleton are clearly related to other canids. Furthermore, many of the communication and food-gathering behaviors of red foxes are typical of canids: well-developed food-caching behavior, extensive scavenging behavior, hunting strategies, a well-developed pair bond where both parents help to raise the young, den digging, and a strong dominance hierarchy among females. Members of the cat family, Felidae, show none of these behavioral traits, or show them only to a very limited degree. Yet in my research, I have been struck time and time again by how catlike the red fox is.

A number of fox and small cat species exhibit long catlike vibrissae, or whiskers, on both their muzzles and their wrists (carpal joints). The whiskers of foxes are proportionally longer than those of other canids. They probably function as tactile or touch organs. The muzzle vibrissae may help to guide the fox's capturing and killing bites, and the carpal vibrissae may assist the fox in stalking, or while pinning the prey to the ground with its forepaws. Foxes also have long, thin, but robust canine teeth that resemble the daggerlike canines of cats. Once they have captured a small prey, canid species typically shake their heads vigorously to immobilize and kill the prey. But red foxes and cats do it differently. Instead of using head shaking, they press their long canine teeth into the prey and keep exerting pressure until they damage the prey's central nervous system.

Red foxes also have catlike paws: they can flex and partially retract their front claws. This feature probably evolved as an adaptation to help keep the claws sharp. Foxes and cats are equally well developed in their fine sense of balance. Good balance combined with soft foot pads and feet that are partially fur-covered are all adaptations that increase a predator's ability to stalk. Foxes and small cat species frequently hunt by stalking.

Convergent evolution between the fox and the cat, however, is most striking in the anatomy of their eyes. Both groups of animals have a highly developed tapetum lucidum—the glistening layer of tissue on the innermost sheath of the eyeball. It reflects light back out of the eyes and causes the eyes of foxes and cats to glow a luminous dull green, even though no strong light is shining into them. This membrane acts like a mirror behind the retina, so that light passes over the retina twice instead of once. It is a light multiplying device to increase night vision. Foxes have also evolved a catlike vertically slit pupil that can close down to shut out bright sunlight.

Both red and gray foxes show a lateral threat display similar to the one used by a house cat. When a fox threatens another fox with this display, it stands broadside, arches its back, erects its fur and charges

The fox's catlike whiskers are tactile organs. Functions of the black spots are not clear.

broadside in a stiff-legged run. However, it is during its hunting that the actions of a red fox are most like a cat. When hunting birds or squirrels, the fox stalks with its belly almost touching the ground, or slinks from cover to cover, crouching and waiting for its chance to ambush the prey.

What explanation is there for this parallelism between foxes and cats? My hypothesis is that vulpine foxes separated early from the rest of Canidae and began to show convergent evolution with small wild cat species, while the rest of the Canidae family evolved differently. What ecological selection pressures were guiding the evolution of these similarities? A detailed examination of food sources shows that foxes in general, and red foxes in particular, hunt many of the same kinds of prey as small feline predators. These prey use the same means of escape from both cats and foxes. They run into small burrows or under objects, fly up out of reach, use their highly sensitive sight and hearing to detect approaching predators, and have camouflage coloration and great alertness. To overcome the antipredator devices of their prey, foxes and cats have developed a number of similar features. As a result, the red fox has evolved to become a very catlike canid.

4

The Fox as Hunter

OUT IN FRONT of me 50 yards or so, along the edge of a quiet country roadside, the vixen I had named Amber stopped suddenly. She turned broadside, lifted her head and perked her ears. Then slowly she stalked a few paces off into the long grasses that grow next to the road. Amber tested each foothold, careful not to make a sound. Fixing her eyes on small movements in the grass in front of her, she froze for several seconds. Then she coiled into a deep crouch, waited a moment, adjusted her feet and lunged. She landed as gracefully as she had launched herself, her forepaws touching down where the grass had been moving. Amber tried to pin the mouse to the ground, but it had escaped to a nearby burrow. After a brief search, she returned to the edge of the road and continued to walk down it searching for other prey.

The fox's hunting behavior is one of the most exciting aspects of its life. And, because in forested regions and other densely vegetated areas red foxes often use hiking paths, deer runs and roadsides to hunt

from, there is a good chance that at dawn or dusk you can find red foxes along these trails. Red foxes hunt mainly small animals: mice, voles, songbirds, rabbits and insects, such as beetles and grasshoppers. A red fox may tackle a prey as large as a grouse, ptarmigan or jackrabbit, but larger animals are usually scavenged rather than killed.

In my research, I watched and described the various hunting tactics of red foxes. One problem I faced was when to judge the fox's behavior a serious hunt and when to call it general searching for prey. I knew from reading the articles of other researchers that red foxes usually capture their prey by biting it or by pinning it to the ground with a vigorous forepaw stab. I decided that in my field research one of these "capture motor patterns" had to be present before a behavior was judged to be a "completed hunt." If the motor pattern was not present, the behavior was classified as "searching for prey."

Over the years, I have carefully watched more than 400 completed hunts made by 22 different wild red foxes. Each hunt I valued as if it were a small key unlocking a

Head lifted, ears perked, this red fox fixes its eyes on the movements of a small rodent.

deeper understanding of the fox as predator, and each hunt was studied in detail. Some hunts were filmed and then watched many times. How successful a predator is the red fox? In 139 out of 434 hunts, that is, in 32 percent of these hunts, the fox ended up with prey in its mouth. The foxes either ate the prey immediately or cached it for later use. I also compared how efficient the foxes were at capturing various kinds of prey. The foxes captured small mammals 23 percent of the time (60 out of 257 hunts), birds approximately 2 percent of the time (2 out of 83 hunts) and insects 82 percent of the time (77 out of 94 hunts). What radically different success rates!

What causes these large differences? Insects, such as grasshoppers and crickets, did not show effective escape behaviors from the foxes. If a fox missed capturing one of these prey, the insect often hopped one or two strides away; the fox watched where it landed and was often able to relocate and capture it. At the other end of the scale, songbirds were very successful at escaping. These prey have extremely quick reactions and are very watchful when feeding on the ground, periodically flying up and surveying the area for approaching predators. Small mammals were intermediate in their success at getting away and tried to escape the jaws of hunting foxes by either outrunning the predator (rabbits), fleeing down a burrow or scurrying under a boulder or log (mice, voles and shrews) or climbing trees (red squirrels).

Only during the spring when certain species of ducks and gulls nest on the ground can red foxes effectively capture these birds and their eggs. Several researchers have documented that in gull-breeding colonies, foxes can kill several hundred birds in the course of a single night. However, I know of no researcher who has found birds to be a significant portion of the diet of red foxes on a year-round basis.

How do foxes "perceive" their prey? Does a red fox hunt mammals in one manner, birds differently, and insects with a third hunting strategy? If not, how does a fox respond to the various kinds of prey that it hunts? By analyzing my 434 hunts, I discovered that red foxes group and hunt their quarry according to a classification system only slightly different from our own.

The first prey group consists of insects—prey that foxes hunt in a casual manner.

The second cluster of prey includes small mammals, such as mice, voles, ground squirrels and gophers, but it also includes insectivores (shrews) and animals as large as muskrats. After watching the foxes hunt these mammals, I noted that what these prey have in common, at least from the fox's point of view, is that they escape by fleeing down a burrow or dashing under an object like a rock or fallen tree. Consequently, I labeled this group of prey "small burrowing mammals."

The third cluster of prey includes rabbits, snowshoe hares and jackrabbits. Lagomorphs, as biologists call members of the rabbit family, often flee from the fox by running, and the strategy foxes employ for hunt-

Foxes stalk close to rabbits and then capture them after a hell-bent-for-leather chase.

ing these fleet-footed prey reflects this fact.

The fourth prey group consists of birds and tree squirrels. These prey have keen eyesight, a tendency to flee upwards to escape and an ability to keep watch for predators from high perches. These antipredator strategies help explain certain features evident in the hunting behavior of the fox.

Insects

THE FOXES I STUDIED usually hunted crickets, grasshoppers and beetles, but occasionally captured flies and moths. When you see a fox hunting insects, you will notice that it rarely exhibits the high degree of tension and excitement it shows in hunting other types of prey. The fox's casualness in these hunts is explained by the weakly developed escape behaviors that many insects show, as well as by the fact that foxes only end up with a tidbit of food when they are successful. In addition, foxes usually hunt insects during another activity; that is, they seldom show searching behavior specifically toward insects. In my study area, insects seem to represent snack food that foxes capture along the way.

From what I have seen, foxes usually hunt these prey in a nonchalant manner, snapping at flies or moths that happen to come close to their head. Or a fox may by chance discover a grasshopper that is moving in the grass or leaves. When this opportunity knocks, the fox stops the activity it is engaged in, walks over, bites down, and

chews up the grasshopper, cricket or beetle. Many times the hunt is just as simple as that. Sometimes the fox misses in its initial capture attempt, watches where the in-

With an almost nonchalant manner that reflects the small size of the prey, this fox hunts for an insect.

sect lands, and searches for it by poking its muzzle into shrubs or stamping one of its forefeet on the forest floor where it expects the insect to be.

Red foxes, however, are impressively adaptable in their hunting behavior. If insects or other invertebrates are locally abundant, the foxes will make heavy use of these prey. David Macdonald observed that foxes in the suburbs and farmlands around Oxford, England, regularly harvest earthworms from people's front lawns, and these worms made up a significant portion of the foxes' summertime diet. His study shows that with varying environmental conditions, red foxes can adapt their hunting behaviors. It may be worthwhile to check the parks or local golf course near your home

Head and ears in the telltale "mousing" posture, this fox attempts to locate a small rodent.

after a heavy rain. Earthworm tunnels become flooded and the worms come out on the surface. At these times, you may be able to observe red foxes harvesting them.

The casual demeanor that red foxes exhibit while capturing insects is unique to this type of hunting. At times you may even have difficulty separating insect-hunting behavior from scavenging behavior. However, the other prey that red foxes hunt offer much more challenging contests, with the result that each type of prey is hunted using a distinctive tactic.

Small burrowing mammals

As I have mentioned, one of the best opportunities to observe a red fox hunting is when it is traveling along a game trail, rabbit path, hiking trail or even the edge of a roadside, searching for small burrowing mammals. Fresh fox tracks found along these paths may alert you to the ones the foxes in your area regularly use. Spend some time looking for foxes along these trails, particularly at dusk and dawn.

The fox's strategy for hunting chipmunks, pocket gophers, mice, voles and shrews is considerably more complex than its insect-hunting strategy. In forested areas, the foxes characteristically use paths and trails for two reasons. First, if the trail is wide enough, dense vegetation grows adjacent to it, and small burrowing mammals are frequently abundant in this edge vegetation. Second, foxes appear to use trails for quietness; that is, the fox must approach these prey without itself being detected. If the fox makes a sound, cracking a dried twig or rustling a leaf, the prey will either crouch motionless, making detection difficult, or flee down a burrow or under a log to safety. When the fox is trail-walking in this manner—with its head held high and its ears perked, peering down into grasses and shrubs —I know it is hunting for small burrowing mammals. This elevated head position is so characteristic of small burrowing mammal hunts that I have termed it "head in mousing position."

When a fox locates prey adjacent to the trail, it may lower its head and sniff, or raise its head and then rotate it, cocking it first one way and then the other. These small head movements place the fox's ears at slightly different angles from the suspected prey. It has been demonstrated that red foxes can locate small rustling sounds to within inches of their true location.

Alternatively, the fox may search by stalking off the trail. When the fox stalks small burrowing mammals, it puts its forefeet down carefully so as not to make any sounds. Then the fox stops, elevates its head and cocks it back and forth, searching the spot where it suspects the prey lies. As the fox moves forward, it puts its hind feet exactly where its forefeet have been, thus minimizing any noise. When the fox appears to have located the small burrowing mammal, it crouches deeply and then lunges, arcing through the air. At the end of the lunge, the fox tries to pin the prey to the ground with its forefeet. Then the fox dispatches the prey with several quick bites to the body or carries it off to a safe area and plays with it, very much the way a cat plays with it.

The fox's hunting lunges after small burrowing mammals are normally short (1 to 2 yards or meters), but they can be impressively long. I have observed red foxes, from a standing start on level ground, catapult themselves 16 feet (5 m) through the air and successfully pin prey to the ground. Foxes also frequently hunt on the downhill side of trails. They may do this because by lunging downhill, a greater area is placed within their reach. After observing

several of these graceful and impressive downhill lunges, I made careful measurements and found that these foxes were airborne for up to 28 feet (8.5 m), before stabbing the prey to the ground with their forepaws.

Rabbits and hares

A RED FOX HUNTS lagomorphs with a third strategy: it stalks toward the prey, and then there is a "hellbent for leather" pursuit as the fox tries to capture it. In a typical hunt after a snowshoe hare, the fox crouches low to the ground and moves slowly toward the hare while staring at it intensely. Detecting the fox, the hare suddenly bolts and flees, often through thick cover, while the fox follows in a bounding gallop. When it gets close to the hare, the fox attempts to bite it in the hind leg or rump. Frequently at this point, the hare will suddenly change direction and zigzag to put

In hunting small mammals, foxes often follow paths and trails or travel along roadsides.

distance between itself and the fox. These actions may be repeated, and the chase continues over a fairly large portion of the woods. Every time the fox comes close, the hare zigzags and runs off in a new direction. Finally the snowshoe hare either escapes in dense enough vegetation that the fox cannot follow, or the fox gets a bite-hold on the prey, pulls it off its feet, and pins it to the ground with one or both forelegs. Several quick bites to the head or neck are usually enough to dispatch the hare.

Arboreal prey

WHEN HUNTING BIRDS and tree squirrels, the red fox's strategy again changes dramatically. It is in this type of hunting that foxes appear strikingly catlike. Observe house cats hunting for sparrows and other prey along the edge of backyards and in nearby parks. Describe their behavior in detail. Then when you observe red foxes hunting arboreal prey, you will be able to make your own comparison between these two predators. The similarities are fascinating.

The foxes I studied did not spend time searching for birds or tree squirrels, as they did for small burrowing mammals. Rather, foxes hunt them whenever they encounter them on the ground in a vulnerable position. When a fox spots a bird or tree squirrel, it immediately crouches so low that its belly almost touches the ground, its neck is held horizontal, ears alert, and it remains motionless while staring intently at the prey. The fox often "slink-runs" at the prey, starting with a stalking pace, changing to a trot

and finally breaking into a gallop. The fox maintains its low crouching position throughout the charge. The last part of the slink-run is a horizontal thrust-jump, ending with the fox trying to capture the prey with a bite. The forepaw stab that foxes use for small burrowing mammals is not used when the fox tries to capture birds or tree squirrels.

In most hunts after arboreal prey, the fox stalks in order to get closer to its quarry, and the emphasis in this type of stalking is quite different from the stalking used to capture small burrowing mammals. In hunts after burrowing mammals, the fox puts its feet down slowly and carefully so as not to make any noise; it moves its head around freely, searching for a quiet route and then looking at the place where it suspects the prey to be. When stalking birds or tree squirrels, the fox may make little rustling sounds as its feet move across the ground, but it is always in a deeply crouched posture, and its head and eyes are fixed on the prey as though tied to it by an invisible cord. These two stalking techniques appear to exploit different weaknesses in the prey's defenses. In small mammal hunts, the fox's stalking minimizes noise that might alert the prey. During bird and squirrel hunts, stalking appears designed to minimize visual cues.

When it is hunting arboreal prey, small noises made by the fox are masked by the fox synchronizing its movements exactly to the times when the prey is moving. This same type of synchronization of movements can be observed in house cats as they hunt birds. It suggests that the antipredator devices of ar-

Juvenile fox pups devour a rabbit, most likely caught for them by one of their parents.

boreal prey have dictated how medium-sized predators, such as cats and foxes, must hunt these prey if they wish to succeed. There are only a very limited number of ways to capture these alert, quick animals.

A discriminating predator

THE FACT THAT red foxes use radically different hunting strategies to capture small burrowing mammals and arboreal prey has several interesting ramifications. Remember that red foxes are often hunting these prey in dense vegetation where the prey cannot be seen, only heard. Now consider several points. First, red foxes decide early in a hunt which hunting strategy to use. Second, foxes often make this choice based on only a few rustling sounds that the prey has made. Third, I have seldom observed foxes using an inappropriate hunting strategy—that is, a slink-run strategy on a mouse or vole or a lunging strategy on a bird. All of this suggests that red foxes have highly developed hearing abilities.

Try it for yourself. Close your eyes and listen to a small animal making rustling sounds in tall grasses or dried leaves. Based solely on these sounds, can you decide whether it is a small burrowing mammal or a bird? A fox often has to do exactly that. And in the 434 fox hunts I observed, a fox used an inappropriate hunting tactic in only two. The fox has developed these auditory abilities to an impressive degree.

There are many other aspects of the fox's hunting repertoire waiting to be investigated. We only have a superficial understanding of this exquisite and sophisticated predator. Much remains to be learned.

5

Adaptations of a Hunter

O F T H E F O U R hunting strategies of red foxes, the long hunting lunges they use to capture small burrowing mammals are the most impressive. To watch foxes lunge, tracing an arc through the sunlit air of a summer's evening, is an experience I will not forget. I have often thought about the significance of these lunges and have asked myself: how does the fox perform such graceful feats? How does it arc 25 feet (8 m) through the air, floating over fallen branches and dense bushes, to pin a mouse to the ground exactly at the moment when its forepaws touch down? I realized that in performing one of these graceful hunting lunges, a fox is just like any projectile—be it rocket, bullet or lunging fox—and the physics of a projectile says that there are only four factors that could affect the length of the trajectory: (1) the fox could maximize the length of a lunge by taking off at an angle of 45 degrees to the ground; (2) the muscular force that the fox exerts against the ground before taking flight could be made as great as possible; (3) the

amount of time that the fox exerts this force against the ground could be maximized; (4) the fox could reduce its weight without lessening the power of its lunging muscles.

Angle of attack

D U R I N G M Y F I E L D S T U D I E S, I had filmed foxes making these long lunges. I used a frame-by-frame analyzer to measure the fox's take-off angle and found that the foxes on average take off from the ground at an angle of 40 degrees, plus or minus 6 degrees. The fox is indeed a fairly good marksman, and there may be a good reason why the fox is generally slightly below the optimum value of 45 degrees. The higher the fox goes during the lunge, the more it can be blown around by the wind, and the more likely it is to be seen by the prey. I would expect the fox to use the lowest take-off angle it could and still reach its prey.

Lunging 25 feet through the air, a fox can capture a mouse at the exact moment its forepaws touch down.

Lift-off power

HAVING FOUND some useful information on the first tactic, I decided to look at tactic two (maximizing the *force* against the ground) and tactic three (maximizing the amount of *time* the fox exerts force against the ground). To understand the difference between these two factors, we can look at animals like kangaroos, frogs and rabbits. These are called saltatorial animals, animals specialized for hopping. Saltatorial animals show massively developed hind legs, and they all sit in a deeply crouched position. The muscle mass of their hind legs is impressively developed, and these muscles maximize the force exerted against the ground.

But how kangaroolike is the red fox? It certainly doesn't seem to have the massively developed hind legs. It relies too much on running to have evolved such huge extremities. But could there be more subtle muscular adaptations evolved in the hind limbs of a red fox for increasing the power it exerts against the ground during these hunting lunges? It is a definite possibility, but proving it will require further studies, perhaps by researchers more specialized in anatomy and morphology.

Concerning tactic three—adaptations that a lunging fox uses to increase the amount of time it exerts force against the ground—I found some interesting research. I came across a 20-year-old study by Milton Hildebrand, who had carefully analyzed the body proportions of a number of canid species. He came to the conclusion that red foxes had disproportionately long hind limbs compared to other closely related canid species. Hildebrand said that he did not understand the significance of this characteristic. I suggest the reason this vulpine feature evolved is that foxes lunge from a deeply crouched posture. This deep crouch, combined with their long hind limbs, increases the time that a fox can exert force against the ground and lengthens the range of its hunting lunges.

Efforts to jettison cargo

WHAT ABOUT tactic four? Could the fox reduce its body weight without a loss of muscular power as an adaptation for lengthening the range of its hunting lunges? In the first chapter, I explained that red foxes weigh only about half as much as coyotes or dogs of the same general body proportions. If red foxes are disproportionately light compared to other canids, what mechanisms during evolution have foxes used to lighten their body weight without losing muscular power? What body cargo has the fox been able to jettison in order to become the featherweight of wild canids?

Red foxes have small, light stomachs that correlate well with their bite-sized prey. The largest amount of meat that I have ever seen a fox eat at one sitting is approximately 1.5 pounds (0.7 kg), or about 10 percent of its body weight. By comparison, a wolf consumes 18 to 25 pounds (8 to 11 kg) of meat regularly at one of its kills. This amounts to 20 percent of its body weight. Thus the stomach capacity of wolves is proportionately twice that of red foxes.

Red foxes have disproportionately long hind limbs compared to closely related canid species.

Hildebrand found in his research that red foxes also have a number of bones that are significantly reduced in their relative width as compared to the same bones in other members of the dog family. In red foxes, the sacrum (hip bone), sternum (breast bone), scapulae (shoulder bones), lumber vertebrae (lower back bones), baculum (penis bone), and ulna and fibula (lower leg bones) are all significantly reduced in width, a feature that could contribute to a reduction of body weight. If you ever have a chance to see a fox skeleton in the field or in a museum collection, look at these bones and notice how slender they are.

Also, the limb bones of foxes are lighter than we might expect in a canid species of its size. I did some detailed comparisons between the limb bones of red foxes and coyotes and found that for every gram of bone, the limb bones of coyotes showed 3.88 cm² of surface area, while in red foxes, this value is doubled; namely, for every gram of bone, vulpine limb bones show 6.42 cm² of surface area.

In essence, I believe that the skeleton of the red fox has evolved to reduce the weight of its bones, very much as the skeletons of many bird species have evolved. At the same time, the internal structure of fox bones may have changed so as not to sacrifice strength.

These lunge-lengthening adaptations are undoubtedly useful in other contexts as well. For example, the fox's dart-about running, whether in chasing after rabbits or eluding coyotes, makes use of its light body weight and its long hind limbs. But all of these features definitely come together to help the fox soar quietly aloft and float silently over bushes in order to pin an unsuspecting mouse to the ground.

6

Caching: Setting Food Aside for the Future

THERE ARE TIMES when you can experiment with red foxes. Some of my most exciting moments in the field were when I tested hypotheses about fox behavior using the free-ranging foxes of Prince Albert National Park as my subjects. Niko Tinbergen, one of the founders of ethology (the science of animal behavior), as well as David Macdonald and I all agree that the food-caching and urine-marking behaviors of red foxes offer good opportunities for experimentation. Ethology is an experimental science whose knowledge advances by formulating hypotheses and then testing these hypotheses in well-designed behavioral experiments. The principles of the scientific method apply to all experiments regardless of whether the researcher is trying to split atoms, develop a new vaccine or decipher the message content of a red fox display. In this chapter, I describe some of the experiments that other field researchers and I have carried out on free-ranging red foxes. I encourage you to explore the potential of using this approach. It is a powerful tool for understanding red foxes. Let's begin by looking at their caching behavior.

Storing strategies

UPON RISING from a rest period, a fox normally sets off to hunt or scavenge. These food-gathering activities take up approximately 35 percent of the fox's day. At first, any food obtained through hunting or scavenging is eaten, until the fox's appetite is sated. After this point, the fox often continues to hunt and scavenge, and any additional food that the animal finds is cached for later use.

Working from memory, a fox begins to dig through the forest floor litter to uncover a food item it had previously cached.

I have watched foxes of all ages cache and have probably seen this behavior over 500 times. When a red fox caches, it has a remarkably mechanical look about it. Certain components of caching are performed in a fairly rigid or stereotyped manner. True, there is some variation in how different foxes cache surplus food or even how the same fox caches a piece of bread versus a piece of meat. But this variation is highly predictable, and it is the stereotyped quality of caching behavior that raises some interesting questions.

All the foxes I have studied cache, but I'll describe the behavior of one I call Amber. Normally, Amber carries the food item well away from the place where she obtained it. If Amber discovers several food items at the same location, she typically scatter-hoards this food; that is, she caches each mouthload of food in a separate hole, and the holes will be well spaced from each other. Other animals, such as tree squirrels, larder-hoard their food supplies; that is, the animal places all surplus food in one, or just a few, carefully chosen locations. The red fox, however, is definitely a scatter-hoarder.

Holding the food in her mouth, Amber digs a hole 2 to 4 inches (5 to 10 cm) deep. She digs gently, keeping the excavated dirt close to the edge of the hole. The fox does not spray the dirt back as she digs, but neatly piles it next to the hole. Then, placing the dead prey or other food item in the hole, Amber packs the food down, using the end of her snout. Next she pushes the loose dirt over the food item and firmly packs the soil down, stabbing at it with her snout. She uses her nose much as I would use a blunt stick, pressing the food into the hole and packing dirt on top of it. Finally, again with her snout, Amber rakes leaves and twigs on top of her cache and, with various pokes and jabs, rearranges this forest litter until her cache blends perfectly with the surrounding forest floor. She makes a few final adjustments, lifts her head, looks down at her camouflage and walks away, seemingly confident that she has food tucked away for future use.

On average, a fox takes approximately 90 seconds to dig a hole and cache a food item. However, the time spent caching can vary greatly, depending upon how carefully the fox buries the item, as well as how carefully the fox camouflages the caching spot with leaves or twigs or by brushing snow over the spot during winter.

During lean and hungry times, that is, if hunting turns bad, if a fox injures itself or if heavy weather sets in, a fox relies on its caches. I have found that a fox can maintain itself on approximately one pound (0.5 kg) of meat per day, and I have traveled with foxes on days when most of their daily rations have come from their buried caches.

If you are able to observe free-ranging foxes for any length of time, you will undoubtedly observe foxes caching their surplus food and relocating and eating the caches at a later time. If you are studying foxes mainly by tracking them, it is more difficult to detect their well-disguised caches, but with practice it can be done.

It helps to watch foxes cache food repeatedly. Nobel Prize-winning ethologist

A fox hunts until its appetite is satisfied. If it captures additional food, it is cached. This fox prepares to excavate a hole into which it will place the bird lying in front of its forepaws.

Niko Tinbergen describes this phase of studying an animal's behavior as "exploratory watching." He advises field biologists to watch a behavior many times, until even the idiosyncrasies of the behavior make good practical sense. For just as evolution sculpts and perfects an animal's teeth to suit its diet, so does evolution sculpt the form of a behavior, until it achieves its adaptive function easily and effectively. By watching a behavior over and over, one begins to understand why it has evolved in a specific way. Tinbergen considers this type of animal-watching one of the most difficult and important tasks that a naturalist carries out. Its importance should not be underestimated.

The first few times I watched red foxes cache their surplus food, I wondered, as many naturalists had before me, if the animals ever retrieve these caches. Are they really of any use? How do the foxes ever manage to relocate them? After following foxes for several months, I became impressed with their incredible memory and ability to relocate obscure nooks and crannies on the forest floor. Foxes do remember precisely where they put many of their caches and return to them within a few hours or a few days to consume the contents.

Experimenting with caching

USING HAND-RAISED red foxes in Britain, David Macdonald demonstrated the red fox's capability to remember and relocate its caches. In his experiment, he used Niff, a vixen he has raised almost from birth and whom he can take on long exploratory walks on a leash through the farmlands around Oxford. Over the course of six months while on these walks, Macdonald provided Niff with 50 dead mice, which she cached in 50 different locations. From these caches, usually within a day or two, Niff recovered and ate 48 of the mice—a 96 percent recovery rate.

The next question Macdonald focused on was whether Niff was relocating these caches by memorizing their locations or by sniffing around in roughly the right place and locating the cache from olfactory cues. To explore this question, he ran two field experiments. In the first experiment, every time Niff cached a mouse that she was given, Macdonald hid a second mouse within 3 yards (3 m) of the first cache. He did this at a later time and without Niff being present. In making this artificial cache, Macdonald mimicked as closely as he could Niff's caching behavior: He dug a shallow hole in the soil, packed the mouse in the hole and covered it with several layers of dirt. He then packed the dirt down and disguised the location with twigs and leaves

until all signs that something was buried there seemed to have been obliterated. This creation of artificial foxlike caches is a technique you might want to try on the foxes you are observing. In Macdonald's experiment, Niff located almost 90 percent of her own caches but only discovered 22 percent of the artificial caches.

In the second experiment, Macdonald actually dug up each of Niff's cached mice and reburied it within one yard (1 m) of its original hiding place. This time, Niff found only about 25 percent of the transplanted caches. From these results, Macdonald concluded that Niff principally uses memory, not olfactory clues, to find her caches, and hones in very precisely on their locations.

I do not doubt the results of Macdonald's experiments, nor do I disagree with the conclusions he reached. However, from observing free-ranging red foxes relocate several hundred caches in my study area, I question whether Niff's behavior conveys the whole story of how wild red foxes relocate and use their caches. I have often observed one of my foxes return to a location where food was buried and sniff around in that general area until it relocated the buried cache, apparently using its sense of smell. I have watched a number of foxes find their own caches in this manner as well as sniff out and pilfer caches made by another fox. From all the watching I have done, I concluded that red foxes retrieve buried caches by at least four different mechanisms: (1) most commonly, the fox remembers the exact location where the cache was buried; (2) the fox may remember only the general area where it placed the cache and may locate the food by smell; (3) a fox may simply stumble upon a cache, that is, detect it entirely by smell; (4) a fox may track another fox and detect its caches by smell. Mechanisms (3) and (4) usually result in one fox stealing another fox's caches. However, it is important to remember that foxes exist on family territories: when a cache is stolen by another fox, it is usually a mate or offspring, so the stolen cache is not really wasted. Furthermore, if foxes were "honest," that is, if foxes retrieved only their own caches, the number of mechanisms used for retrieving caches would be cut in half. By using all four retrieval mechanisms and "stealing" caches whenever possible, the number of wasted caches is probably greatly reduced, and each fox on the family territory ends up with more caches than if it had retrieved only its own.

This battery of retrieval tactics helps to explain another idiosyncrasy in the fox's caching behavior. In the hundreds of times that I have observed red foxes cache, high-quality foods (like pieces of meat or freshly killed prey) are always buried so that they are covered by only 2 to 4 inches (5 to 10 cm) of dirt. During wintertime, these high-quality items are buried under 2 to 4 inches of snow. If red foxes always retrieved their

The fox's final step in caching is to use its nose to carefully rake leaves and debris over the hole until the site blends perfectly with its surroundings, *top*. *Bottom:* the cache's contents uncovered.

After a successful hunt, a fox carries its prey off to find a suitable place to bury it.

buried caches simply by remembering where they were, then the depth the food was buried would be unimportant. However, I believe that mechanism (2)—remembering the general area of the cache and then relying on smell—helps to explain why the items are buried shallowly. The paw-depth burial of food items represents a compromise in a difficult situation. On the one hand, the fox has to bury its food deep enough so that scavenging mammals (such as weasels, coyotes and bears) and scavenging birds (such as ravens, crows and jays) that could rob the fox's caches are foiled. On the other hand, the fox does not want to bury it so deep that it cannot sniff it out if the exact location is forgotten. A thin blanket of dirt or snow on top of the cached food seems to be a good compromise.

Cutting one's losses

THERE ARE MANY other intriguing aspects of the red fox's caching behavior that can be explored by a naturalist using an experimental approach. Why do foxes consistently spread their caches out, putting food items in separate, well-spaced holes? The consensus among field biologists is that the fox cuts its losses by scattering its caches. A reasonable assumption—or hypothesis—is that spreading caches out over

80

the family territory makes them harder for pilfering scavengers to find.

I decided to test this hypothesis, and by relating my set-up in some detail, I hope to offer you the ability to design field experiments of your own. The results you can end up with are fascinating.

I carried out this experiment in a wilderness area of Saskatchewan's Prince Albert National Park. This pristine area contains many animals that probably pilfer the caches of a fox if given a chance—animals as large as black bears, wolves and coyotes and as small as Canada jays, shrews and beetles. On the first day of my experiment, I hiked a long way into this wilderness forest. In my backpack, I had a good supply of canned dog food, and in one of my pockets, I had four wood chips, each with a different instruction printed on it. I shuffled these chips and pulled one out at random. If the chip said "larder," I proceeded to larder-cache the dog food. Specifically, I placed 9 chunks of dog food in the same hole and buried this meat under 4 inches (10 cm) of dirt. I carefully packed the dirt down in several tight layers with my fingertips and proceeded to disguise the spot as skillfully as I could with leaves and litter.

I then hiked down the trail a mile and a half and off into the forest on one side. I shuffled the remaining wood chips in my pocket and pulled one out. If it said "three," each chunk of dog food on this plot was placed in a different hole, and the holes were separated from each other by approximately 3 yards (3 m). I dug each hole 3 to 4 inches (5 to 10 cm) deep, placed the food in the bottom of the hole, packed the dirt carefully over the top of it and disguised the spot. I repeated this artificial caching behavior 9 times in

In the winter, a fox uses snow to disguise its cache as effectively as it does in the summer.

that location until all the chunks of dog food were set up in a tidy square plot.

Again I hiked down the trail the same distance and off to the other side. I had two wood chips remaining in my pocket. If I pulled out the one that said "15," I laid out a square plot of 9 dog food caches in exactly the same manner as before except this time they were separated from each other by approximately 15 yards (14 m).

And again, down the trail the required distance and off to the other side, I pulled the last wood chip out and it said "75." The same kind of plot was set up, except the "inter-cache distance" was increased this time to 75 yards (68 m). My hypothesis behind all this was that if scattering the caches reduced the average number of caches lost to pilfering animals, then the more scattering the better. In other words, by increasing the distance between caches, I should find a decrease in the number of caches lost to pilfering animals.

I made detailed field notes in order to remember the location of each of these caches. I left all the caches in place for a week and hoped that I could relocate them after that time. I decided that I should replicate the experiment 15 different times. It had taken me four hours to construct the original plot, but I spent the next couple of days working from five in the morning until midnight, setting out this huge supply of dog food. After a week, I revisited each cache and evaluated what had taken place. The scavengers of this wilderness area cooperated beautifully, and interesting results began to roll in.

Five of the 15 larder-hoarded caches had been devastated; every bit of food had been cleaned out of these holes. The other 10 larder-hoarded caches were in perfect shape, well-preserved and undetected by any pilfering animal. How did this compare with the other caching techniques? For the 3-yard plots, an average 7 out of 9 caches survived. For the 15-yard caching plots, an average of 6.47 out of 9 survived, and for the 75-yard plots, an average of 7.27 out of 9 survived. Lining these averages up—6.00, 7.00, 6.47, and 7.27—showed that there was no consistent increase in the survival of the caches as they were spaced further apart. However, I knew from personal experience that scatter-caching is considerably more work than larder-caching. So what benefit does the fox gain from making the considerable effort to scatter-cache its surplus food?

I wrestled with these puzzling results for a long time. The experiment had disproved my original hypothesis, and I was at a loss to come up with any alternative idea. The only idiosyncrasy I noticed was that when I larder-hoarded the meat, I experienced an all-or-none loss. If a larder cache was detected at all by a scavenger, I lost everything. If the cache was not detected, my losses were zero. With this type of caching, my luck was either extremely good or extremely bad.

I began to see that regardless of how a fox caches, it seems destined to lose approximately a third of its caches to pilfering animals. Because the fox can do little about this damage, the only question to

With food in its mouth, a fox searches for a secure place to cache it on the edge of a lake.

consider is: can these losses be made more regular and thus more predictable and easier to cope with?

I then measured the variation among my losses. I used a standard deviation formula to calculate how individual results varied around the average. My larder-hoarded caches had all-or-none losses and produced a high standard deviation. On the other hand, the losses for widely spread caches were more moderate, and the standard deviation was smaller.

When I larder-hoarded my caches, an average of 6 pieces of meat survived the week, give or take about 4. I considered that quite a lot of variation. When I scattered the caches 75 yards apart, an average of about 7 of these caches survived, give or take about 1.5. In essence, my experiment showed that by widely scattering the caches, I had cut the variations in my losses to about a third—a

significant improvement.

It seems that by scattering its caches, the fox regulates its losses. The survival of its caches becomes more predictable, and thus the chance that a reliable portion of the caches will be there during a period of food shortages is increased. I had found that my original hypothesis was wrong and that the actual management of cache losses is more subtle and sophisticated than I had first realized.

Field experiments like these are considerable work, but they are exciting. The results unfold with the intrigue of detective work. You don't need to live in a national park or have a hand-raised fox in order to try such a study. If you are a student, make an independent science project out of it, or do it just for the adventure. This kind of field work has given me some of my most rewarding moments as a biologist.

7

Getting That Long-Distance Feeling

ANOTHER REALM that offers great potential for field study is the urine-marking behavior of red foxes. A field biologist on skis or snowshoes can collect urine marks left by canids in fresh snow, keep them frozen in small bottles or vials, and thus have urine marks from different foxes—or from wolves, coyotes or other animals—that can be used in behavioral experiments.

Some people find this strange work. I have had up to a hundred urine marks, each carefully frozen in its own glass vial, each with its own individual label, each carefully stacked up in our basement freezer. During breeding season, the urine marks of red foxes take on a strong odor, and so do I when I collect them. Every dog I pass either gives me a strange look or growls at me. The reception I get from my wife and daughter upon arriving home is not much better, but the scent washes off with a shower or two. It is part of being a fox watcher, and in fact I feel proud when I wear the slightly skunky odor.

Of course, it is not just the urine that I am collecting. Urine·marks of many animals contain by-products of metabolism and glandular secretions that these animals release for the purpose of chemical communication. This form of communication offers a rich cluster of signals and messages that other animals of the same species can decipher, but it is a form of communication that humans have difficulty appreciating. Chemicals that are released into the air or water or onto the ground by one animal in order to stimulate a behavioral response in other individuals of the same species are called pheromones, and there is no doubt that the urine marks of red foxes contain important pheromones.

From tracks in the snow, you will usually be able to identify the species of animal,

Solitary animals by nature, red foxes still must communicate with each other.

and sometimes the sex of the animal, that left the urine mark. In addition, the older the urine mark is, the darker it becomes due to the oxidation of chemicals in the urine. After a while, you will be able to tell whether a urine mark is a fresh one or several days old.

For field experiments, it is probably best to collect fresh urine marks so that the pheromones are still fairly active. To collect a urine mark, I simply hold a clean glass vial next to the urine mark and, with a clean spoon (one purchased for the occasion, not borrowed from the kitchen drawer), shovel the urine-soaked snow into the vial. The vial is tightly capped and labeled with a number that won't fall off, fade or get rubbed off. In my field notebook, I record the species and sex of the animal that made the urine mark and any other relevant information gleaned from having tracked the animal. I use a lot of snow to scrub the spoon after each use. The vial is stored in a backpack so the urine stays frozen in the field, and at home, as soon as I can, I freeze the vial to keep the urine mark as fresh as possible.

Experimenting with urine marks offers rich possibilities for testing hypotheses concerning the natural behavior of red foxes. It has been suggested that red foxes urine-mark the boundaries of their territories so that other foxes can tell whether an area is already occupied. In social encounters, red foxes appear to use urine marking as a dominance display: the dominant fox sometimes urine-marks its mate or a subordinate animal that is cowering in front of it. During breeding season, the males of many species, including foxes, use urine marks deposited by females as a way of locating the females and evaluating their estrous status. Most members of the dog family, and certainly foxes, use urine marks to provide that "long-distance feeling"; that is, urine marks are left behind to inform other foxes about the sex, age, dominance status and perhaps the individual identity of the marker.

These "social information posts" are carefully investigated and then urine-marked by almost every fox that passes by, and the same small landmark (rock, stump, grass tussock) may be an active social post for a number of years. Anyone who regularly walks a dog around a neighborhood has probably observed this important type of canid scent communication.

Like other members of the dog family, foxes use urine marks as "social information posts" so other foxes can tell if an area is occupied.

From observing dogs or foxes, several naturalists have concluded that the pheromones in a urine mark are active for about two or three days (perhaps longer if the weather is colder). It is common to see these canids urine-mark their scent posts again to "freshen" them after several days have passed.

There are still other functions for urine marking. In fact, two schools of thought have arisen among ethologists about the way these marks are used. One group maintains that specific functions for urine marks (marking territories, use as a dominance display or evaluation of breeding status) have evolved in the behavior of the species. The other group maintains that in animal species that are gifted with keen noses, what evolves is a global comprehension that marking substances are useful in many contexts, and there is an ever-expanding list of how these marking substances are used. Which school of thought, or what combination of these two schools, is correct for each species of animal may be sorted out by future research—it is a challenging and important topic in ethology.

Foxes also use urine marks as a bookkeeping system to note where food has already been eaten.

Field testing urine marks

DAVID MACDONALD, with his captive-raised vixen, Niff, demonstrated some of the communication that takes place when red foxes urine-mark. When Niff was about 10 weeks old and they began taking walks in the Oxford countryside, Macdonald observed that at certain places Niff would sniff at the ground and become extremely excited, begin shrieking, prostrate herself on her side and lash her tail about madly. Previous to the next leash walk with Niff, David placed token urine marks, that is, a few drops of urine collected from other captive foxes, on the path and led Niff past these spots. She repeatedly showed the same excited response, and from these results, he was able to show that it was in-

When scavenging, a fox holds its nose just above the ground, and "hoovers" back and forth.

deed the urine marks of other foxes that were the principal cause of the strong submissive behavior shown by his young vixen.

Macdonald then wanted to test whether foxes can identify different individuals solely from their urine marks. By digging up some of Niff's regularly scent-marked tussocks of grass, he could create scent-marking posts made by her, both inside and outside her territory. Using urine obtained from other foxes, he could also create foreign scent posts. When Niff was off her territory and detected a scent mark of a foreign

fox, the scent mark caused her to wheel around, curve her tail anxiously beneath her, and retreat back onto her territory. When she detected one of her own scent marks outside of her territory, she exhibited what can be best described as foxy puzzlement. Her nose "hoovered" the scent mark and the surrounding area as if searching for an explanation of how her odor ended up there. After prolonged sniffing, she did not urine-mark but continued on her way. By contrast, Macdonald observed that when Niff was on her own territory and encountered one of her own marks, she almost invariably left a fresh urine mark after a brief investigation.

Furthermore, Macdonald found that each time he placed the urine mark of a foreign fox on Niff's territory, she investigated it for a prolonged period of time and then repeatedly urine-marked it. In fact, he found that by placing the urine mark of foreign foxes on a log or clump of grass intermittently over a two-week period, he could create a "social information post" that Niff repeatedly investigated and scent-marked every time she passed.

A fox's bookkeeping system

IN RED FOXES, scavenging behavior looks remarkably different from most of the fox's behaviors. In hunting, for example, the fox is either walking quietly down a path or trail with its head, ears and neck in "mousing position," or the fox is crouched low behind a shrub, trying to ambush a prey. When scavenging, the fox holds its nose just above the ground and "hoovers" along, crisscrossing back and forth a number of times in the same area of meadow or patch of woods. In all this crisscrossing, the fox is searching with its eyes and nose for the occasional edible berry, a slow-moving worm or insect, or even caches that other foxes have made. An interesting characteristic in the behavior of my foxes is that scavenging and hunting are seldom mixed; the two activities are clearly separated in time. (Insect hunting is the one exception to this. It looks a good deal like scavenging behav-

ior, and the two activities are often carried out together.)

Another characteristic about scavenging behavior is the incredible amount of urine marking that foxes do during it. I observed a fox urine-mark up to 70 times per hour while scavenging. I became intrigued by what functions were being served by all this urine marking, and it turned into quite an adventure into the olfactory world of the red fox.

Only 12 percent of the urine marks that foxes deposit when scavenging look like they can be interpreted as either territorial urine marks or "social post" urine marks. What was going on with all the other urine marks that the foxes were leaving?

Again I relied on Tinbergen's "exploratory watching" technique, and for several months I simply observed the foxes and tried to keep an open mind about what functions were being served by their scent marking. At some point during that time, it occurred to me that a fox might be keeping track of where it had investigated for food by urine-marking those locations. I wondered if what I was observing was the fox's "bookkeeping system."

I discovered that red foxes, while scavenging, were investigating up to 220 spots per hour, and they were typically scavenging for approximately five hours a day. Thus, while scavenging, a red fox investigates an extremely large number of spots on the forest floor, many more than it could possibly remember without some type of external signal. I also found that after several days, foxes would often scavenge in the same area. I hypothesized that urine marking may function as a type of bookkeeping system during scavenging behavior. A fox urine-marks places where food has already been eaten, but where food odor or food

Urine-marked areas are visited by any passing fox. After sniffing, it will leave a mark of its own.

remnants remain. When the same or a different fox reinvestigates this spot, the scent of fox urine signals "no food," and the fox investigates the spot for only a brief period of time. This use of urine marking might increase the efficiency of the red fox's scavenging behavior so that more food items are found per hour of time spent scavenging.

I was at first skeptical of such a chemical accounting system, but because my hypothesis was generated out of a great deal of exploratory watching, I decided it was worth testing. One prediction that would be easy to test was: red foxes should consistently urine-mark places on the ground where no food occurs but where there are food odors or inedible food remnants. I decided to test seven different substances—gasoline, oil, synthetic urea, trimethylamine, water, canned dog food and dry granular dog food— for their abilities to elicit urine-marking behavior. The first four substances presented the fox with strong odors, but ones that were not food related. I included water in my experiment as a control because it is has very little odor. The two kinds of dog food were included to provide food cues, and they were used as follows: both were placed on the ground in small 1-ounce (30 g) piles. When the fox ate the dry granular dog food, few crumbs and very little odor remained on the ground. On the other hand, when the fox ate the canned dog food, the sign of food and odor did remain on the ground after the fox had eaten. To ensure that this happened, every time I set out canned dog food I smeared some of it against a hard object, such as a rock, tree root or packed soil, immediately next to where I placed the food. The smeared portion, which the fox could not consume, created an "inedible food remnant."

Once every hour as I was following the foxes, I randomly chose one of these seven substances and placed it on the ground a short distance from the animal. The fox usually investigated the substance and ate any food that was present. I recorded whether the fox had urine-marked or not. I continued the experiment for the better part of a month until each of these substances had been presented to the foxes 30 times. Three different foxes participated in the experiment, and they each showed the same patterns. The results are detailed in the accompanying chart.

Clearly only one item—the canned dog food—was consistently urine-marked by the foxes. They seldom urine-marked the granular dog food or any of the strong non-food odors or the water. The soft dog food was also the only item that left the odor and sign of food on the ground. My curious "bookkeeping hypothesis" had survived its first test.

It took me three additional, fairly complicated experiments to test my hypothesis. I have described this work in detail elsewhere (see Recommended Reading, page 103). What began as a hunch, generated by lots of exploratory watching, has turned out to be a newly discovered function for urine marking exhibited by red foxes. Other researchers have found that wolves and coyotes use similar urine-mark systems.

There are many other aspects of fox behavior that can be investigated either by creating artificial fox-like caches or by experimenting with urine-marking behavior. David Macdonald and I have done much to get this experimental approach off the ground. I know I can speak for both of us when I say we would be delighted to see other naturalists and field biologists use this laborious, but satisfying, experimental approach to understanding the behavior of wild foxes.

Bookkeeping by Scent

Three different red foxes showed highly similar patterns in their tendencies to mark certain test substances with urine.

	Times Urine-Marked	Times Not Urine-Marked
Canned dog food	23	7
Dry dog food	4	26
Trimethylamine	1	29
Gasoline	0	30
Oil	3	27
Synthetic urea	0	30
Water	1	29

8

Return of
The Swift Fox

OX SPECIES VARY widely in their ability to cope with the modern world. The red fox, *Vulpes vulpes,* has been very successful in adapting to the habitat changes and pollution problems caused by human societies. The swift fox, *Vulpes velox,* has endured hardship. Why has one fox species prospered while the other has suffered? After examining this question, we will look at the tremendous efforts that have been made to bring the swift fox back from the verge of extinction.

The globe-trotting red fox

THE RED FOX is the most widely distributed carnivore alive in the world today. *Vulpes vulpes* lives on every continent and is expanding its range in the Arctic Islands of northern Canada, the tundra of Siberia, the thorn forests of the Middle East and the arid grasslands of central Australia. It is remarkably adaptable and successful.

Over the past several centuries, humans have wrought numerous changes to the natural environments of the Earth, and many of these changes have had detrimental effects on wildlife. Norman Myers, a conservation biologist who has worked in Africa and Asia, estimates that wildlife may be going extinct at the rate of one species per day. But a few highly adaptable species actually prosper in their interactions with humans. The red fox is one of those. Why?

One important reason is that red foxes thrive in "broken country," that is, in forested country with a patchwork of openings in it. Because of this trait, they have benefited from many of the alterations that humans have made to the landscape. Farming, pasture clearing, timber clear-cutting; the building of houses, golf courses and parks; the construction of roads, airports and suburbs—these are some of the activities that tend to create grassy openings in forested environments. Red fox populations often increase in these areas. As a result,

A small, beautiful grasslands creature, the swift fox has fared poorly in proximity to humans.

there are probably more red foxes alive today than at any other time in history.

Swift but not swift enough

UNFORTUNATELY, certain other fox species, like the swift fox, do not prosper when they are forced to interact with humans. The swift fox, *Vulpes velox*, is a small, beautiful grasslands fox, approximately half the size of a red fox. It has a buff to grayish coat with orange-colored legs and flanks. Swift foxes have the same slender features and light body proportions as the red fox, but they sport a black tip on the end of their tails and have black nose patches.

The swift fox inhabits the grasslands region of North America. Originally it extended from Texas to Alberta and from the Mississippi River west to the foothills of the Rocky Mountains. However, since settlers began to homestead the Prairies in the late 1800s, the species has suffered, and its range has decreased continually. A number of factors have caused the disappearance of this animal from many parts of its former range. In the mid and late 1800s, the swift fox was heavily trapped for its soft, attractive pelt. Also, for much of this century, predator-control programs for wolves and coyotes used bait laced with strychnine. Unfortunately, the poisoned bait was also attractive to swift foxes. In addition, wheat soaked in strychnine has been used for years to control gophers and prairie dogs on farms and ranches. Because strychnine is a stable poison that is not metabolized inside an animal's body, when a rodent dies from this pesticide and is then eaten by a fox, the fox consumes all the poison in the rodent. If the fox scavenges several of these rodents, it does not take long for the fox to accumulate a lethal dose.

One pattern often observed in conservation biology is that animal species frequently survive best in the center of their geographic distribution. This is exactly what happened with swift foxes. Even today, they have stayed relatively numerous in northeastern Colorado and central Wyoming. Towards the periphery of their range, swift foxes have often suffered local extinction. For example, in Canada, the last wild swift fox was sighted in 1938 near the town of Manyberries in southeastern Al-

In the mid to late 1800s, the swift fox was trapped for its soft, attractive pelt.

berta. Swift foxes were not seen again on the Canadian prairies for almost 50 years, until a major wildlife program in the early 1980s was set up to reestablish the species.

Reintroducing the swift fox

THE RETURN of the swift fox to the Canadian prairies is an interesting conservation saga. It was not government agencies or university researchers who initiated the reestablishment of the swift fox, it was two private citizens, Miles and Beryl Smeeton. The Smeetons, originally from England, settled in the foothills of the Canadian Rockies. They conceived the idea of breeding swift foxes in captivity with the hope of reintroducing them to the Canadian prairies. In 1975, they used their life savings to establish the Wildlife Reserve of Western Canada and began to interest researchers, wildlife managers and politicians in their project. After Beryl and Miles died (in 1981 and 1987 respectively), the Wildlife Reserve was first run by Pauline Rhodes and is now under the direction of the Smeetons' daughter, Cleo.

Starting in 1978, many professionals and volunteers contributed to making the Swift Fox Reintroduction Project a success. Wildlife biologists Stephen Herrero of the University of Calgary and Lu Carbyn of the Canadian Wildlife Service oversaw the project. Lawyers volunteered their time to examine provincial wildlife policies and obtain legal permits for the research. Veterinarians contributed by improving the design of captive-breeding facilities, inoc-

ulating swift foxes against disease and quarantining animals when necessary. Geneticists helped by planning a balanced breeding program so that the healthiest possible animals could be released on the Canadian plains. Artists produced beautiful paintings of the swift fox for publicity posters. For fundraising, interested volunteers were brought together to form the Swift Fox Conservation Society, which spearheads the public-education campaign for the conservation of prairie wildlife. Through the Adopt-a-Fox program, individuals and school classes make donations to "adopt" one particular swift fox and are supplied with regular updates on how their fox is doing in the study area.

Today, wildlife biologists not only need to have a sound grasp of biology and ecology, but they also have to be able to work well with people from diverse backgrounds. They need to coordinate all of these efforts in order to accomplish the ecological, educational and political goals of modern conservation programs. An active illustration of these principles can be seen in the milestones of the Swift Fox Recovery Program.

Soft release, hard release

THE FIRST experimental release of swift foxes was carried out in 1983, turning some of the Smeetons' captive-raised animals out onto the arid, gently rolling prairies in southern Alberta. A detailed habitat assessment had been carried out showing that this area would still be suitable. Herrero, Joanne Reynolds and Miles Scott-Brown followed a careful plan. Six pens, approximately 4 by 8 meters (4.4 yards by 8.7 yards), were constructed at widely spaced locations on the prairies. The foxes were housed in these pens over the winter and

Wheat poisoned with strychnine was used to control rodents like this Richardson's ground squirrel. Swift foxes that ate the poisoned rodents died too.

fed daily. The theory behind this "soft release" technique was that by familiarizing the foxes with the site, they would form an attachment to it and stay in the area. All the foxes were equipped with radio-collars so that their movements could be monitored. They were released from the pens in one of two ways: If they had not given birth to a litter, they were let go during early spring. If they had, release was postponed until early fall. After release, supplemental food was set out for one to six months.

The first problem that arose with the soft-release technique was that it was in-

credibly labor intensive. Normally, there was only one researcher working full-time in the field, and almost all of his or her time was used for traveling between the pens and providing food for the foxes. The radio tracking also proved to be extremely time consuming. A second, and more important, problem was that these foxes, once released, often died. Foxes, at best, are a vulnerable species; 40 percent mortality in a fox population is quite normal. Soft-released swift foxes were experiencing 65 percent mortality during the first year on the prairies.

By 1987, it had become clear to Charles Mamo, who had become the main field researcher for the project, that the soft-release technique simply did not get enough foxes out there to build up a stable population. So a change to a hard-release technique was initiated.

This change involved breeding many more captive foxes. By 1987, the Calgary Zoo and the Moose Jaw Wild Animal Park had joined the Wildlife Reserve of Western Canada, and all were breeding foxes. In total, 50 to 60 kits per year could be produced. The hard-release technique consisted of transporting these young foxes, sometimes when they were 4 months old and other times when they were nearly 12 months old, out to the southern Alberta area or the Alberta-Saskatchewan border area and releasing them in the best swift fox habitat that could be identified. No pens. No supplemental feeding. Just open the

HOW TO SPOT A FOX

cages and let the foxes begin their life on the range. Stephen Herrero described the difference in techniques as a matter of "addressing the numbers game. It appeared that we had to get more foxes out there to get past the fairly high mortality rate, in order to establish a small core of foxes on their native habitat."

Another breakthrough in the project came as a result of the almost countless hours that Mamo spent monitoring the swift foxes in the field. He gradually came up with the hypothesis that the release technique may not be as important as the characteristics of the habitat into which the foxes are introduced. Mamo described three habitat characteristics that he felt were crucial to the foxes' survival.

First, there should be good escape terrain; that is, there should be abundant badger holes on the release area so that the captive-raised swift foxes could escape from predators like coyotes, eagles and human hunters. These predators are the foxes' main cause of mortality.

Second, at the time of release, there should be an abundance of easily captured prey in the release area. The prey that is easiest for the foxes to capture is grasshoppers. These captive-raised foxes had not had to hunt for their food, and it took time for them to learn how to capture prey in the wild. If there were abundant grasshoppers at the site, it would help the foxes survive their first couple of months.

Third, there should be a low density of predators, especially coyotes, in the release area. Systematic observation of how many coyotes inhabited certain sites became an important criterion in determining where to release the foxes.

Following Mamo's guidelines, the hard-release technique began to show better field results almost immediately. During the

Researcher Charles Mamo holds a soon-to-be-released swift fox whose movements will be tracked with a radio telemetry collar.

spring of 1988, Mamo reported that some of the swift foxes on the study area had bred and were raising kits of their own. Everyone

A captive-raised swift fox takes its first steps toward freedom on the open prairie.

was most encouraged. However, the good news was short-lived. A harsh drought during the summer and fall of 1988, followed by a severe winter, devastated the fragile population. These conditions caused almost 100 percent mortality among the foxes released that year. That was a very discouraging time for the project. After five years of intense field work, few foxes were alive on the prairies.

However, 1988 appeared to be the darkness before the dawn. The summers of 1989 and subsequent years were wetter. More rain meant better growth of grass, which translated into many more gophers, grasshoppers and other prey that the swift foxes could capture. The hard-release technique continued to establish a greater number of foxes on the study area, and these foxes have raised an increasing number of litters of their own. A sense of cautious optimism has returned to the project.

In 1989, the swift fox researchers were drawn together into a formal Swift Fox Recovery Team. This team began to formulate plans to release swift foxes in other areas, such as the newly established Grasslands National Park in southern Saskatchewan. The team also decided to test a very different approach to releasing them.

Captive-born or wild-born?

DURING THE PAST several years, the Swift Fox Recovery Team has been comparing the survival of swift foxes raised in captivity with the survival of wild foxes captured in central Wyoming or northeastern Colorado. The question being asked is: Do wild-born foxes survive better on the Canadian prairies than captive-raised foxes?

In Wyoming and Colorado, swift foxes are so abundant that the game agencies of these states have always allowed swift foxes to be trapped and their pelts to be sold commercially. By starting this new release program—actually a capture-and-transfer program—the Swift Fox Recovery Team is using these abundant swift foxes for conservation purposes, while at the same time offering the local trappers better economic return for their expertise in live-trapping the foxes. To test whether the wild-born

Swift foxes reestablished on their former haunts have begun to breed.

foxes would survive better than the captive-raised animals, a similar number of radio-collared foxes from each group were released, and their survival was monitored over the next 12 months.

Researchers have now carried out four different releases, two in the spring and two in the fall, each release involving 10 or 20 captive-raised and the same number of wild American-born foxes. The results have been instructive. At the end of a 12-month period, 47 percent of the wild foxes still survived while only 11 percent of the captive-raised foxes were alive. Essentially the same pattern has been repeated in each of the four releases. The team believes that the difference in survival is due to the fact that wild foxes have had a year or more of experience surviving in their natural habitat of

Wyoming or Colorado. They know how to recognize predators and how to avoid life-threatening situations; they know how to capture prey and how to cope with the severe weather conditions often found on the prairies. Captive-raised foxes, when they are released, possess little of this practical experience.

The swift fox project has clearly been a learn-as-you-go effort. Not only has the release technique changed from soft to hard, but the researchers now know that the best survival rates are found in releasing wild rather than captive-raised foxes.

On the other hand, it may not always be possible or appropriate to capture swift foxes in Wyoming and release them in Alberta or Saskatchewan. So the team is now studying how the captive-breeding facilities

Two swift foxes stand outside the kennels used to transport them to their native prairie.

can be redesigned in order to better mimic conditions that the foxes experience in the wild. Working with me, Shelley Pruss and Richard Burton have completed a two-year study of how swift foxes raise their young in the wild. These observations should help to redesign the captive-breeding facility in order to increase swift fox survival.

The amount of time that the parents spend with the kits during each stage of their upbringing and the age at which the pups try different types of wild food have been carefully recorded. Mimicking these natural patterns as closely as possible in the captive-breeding programs—for example, by providing young foxes with live prey (grasshoppers at first, followed by mice and then gophers) at appropriate times in their development—can perhaps provide these young foxes with some experiences that will help them survive better on the open prairie.

A fragile success

WHAT DOES the Swift Fox Recovery Team have to show for all its toil and dedication? There now is a population of approximately 150 to 250 swift foxes established in the Alberta-Saskatchewan border area, and the fox population is growing at an impressive rate, all on its own. In 1991, 18 different pairs of foxes were seen to raise 56 pups. Litter sizes averaged about four kits per litter, a healthy average for any swift fox population. The team now be-

lieves that there are the beginnings of a stable population of swift foxes on the Canadian prairies.

It is still a fragile population. The prairies of North America have changed remarkably during the course of the last century. The great herds of bison have disappeared, the Plains grizzly and prairie wolf have been exterminated, and the land has largely been given over to prairie agriculture. The Canadian prairies are one of the most altered landscapes to be found on the face of the Earth. However, this team of researchers has shown that the swift fox can survive on the prairies of today. Research will continue, and efforts will focus on establishing swift fox populations in two other areas of the Canadian prairies.

Certainly one of the great lessons for us to take from this project is just how difficult it is to reestablish a wildlife population once it has been wiped out of a portion of its original range. Of course species that go entirely extinct can never be replaced. But the research on the swift fox teaches us a more subtle, but equally valuable, lesson: when a wildlife species is removed from just a portion of its range, it may mean a decade or more of concentrated work and hundreds of thousands of dollars to reestablish that species in that area. We must learn to care for what we have, to be responsible for our wildlife. Once lost to an area, a species' reestablishment becomes difficult, even prohibitive. That is the real message the swift fox offers to all of us.

Recommended Reading

I F YOU WISH to learn more about red foxes, you will enjoy the first two books cited below. Taken together, they survey what scientists understand about red fox behavior and ecology in a wide range of environments. On the one hand, David Macdonald principally studied red foxes in the United Kingdom, using hand-raised foxes, foxes that live in suburban and agricultural areas and foxes from wilder areas. David Henry principally studied red foxes in a completely protected environment, Prince Albert National Park in western Canada. Henry's book contains an extensive bibliography.

Henry, J.D. 1986. *Red Fox: The Catlike Canine,* 174 pages: Smithsonian Institution Press, 470 L'Enfant Plaza, Ste. 7100, Washington, D.C. 20560.

Macdonald, D.W. 1987. *Running with the Fox.* London: Unwin Hyman Limited.

224 pages. (Available in the U.S. and Canada from Facts on File, Inc., 460 Park Avenue S., New York, New York 10016.)

Other worthwhile books on canids or wildlife-research techniques include:

Allen, D. 1979. *Wolves of Minong: Their Vital Role in a Wild Community.* Boston: Houghton Mifflin Co.
An excellent book about the ecology and behavior of wolves. Illustrates just how different red foxes are from wolves.

Burt, W.H. and R. Grossenheider. 1974. *A Field Guide to the Mammals.* The Peterson Field Guide Series. Boston: Houghton Mifflin Co.
One of a number of good field guides available for identifying wild mammals.

Chapman, J.A. and G.A. Feldhamer, eds. 1982. *Wild Mammals of North Amer-*

ica: Biology, Management and Economics. Baltimore: The John Hopkins University Press.

One of the best reference works on the taxonomy, ecology, behavior and management of North American mammals.

Murie, O.J. 1974. *A Field Guide to Animal Tracks*. The Peterson Field Guide Series. Boston: Houghton Mifflin Co..

There are other good field guides for identifying animal tracks, but no observations are more careful than Olaus Murie's.

Schemnitz, S.D., ed. 1980. *Wildlife Management Techniques Manual: Fourth Edition, Revised*. Washington, D.C.: The Wildlife Society.

A valuable reference book on wildlife management research techniques. Some people refer to it as the bible on this particular topic. Large public libraries or university libraries should have a copy.

Smeeton, M. 1980. *Completely Foxed*. Toronto: Van Nostrand Reinhold.

Chronicles the efforts of Beryl and Miles Smeeton to establish the Wildlife Reserve of Western Canada and reintroduce the swift fox to the Canadian prairies.

Photography and Illustration Credits

FRONT OF BOOK
page 6, AllStock/Johnny Johnson; page 8, First Light/Brian Milne; page 11, Animals Animals/Johnny Johnson

CHAPTER 1
page 14, AllStock/Tim Davis; page 15, AllStock/Darrell Gulin; page 16, Animals Animals/Michael Leach; page 17, J.D. Henry; page 18, J.D. Henry; page 19, top, J.D. Henry; page 19, bottom, J.D. Henry; page 20, Heather K. Lenz; page 21, Paul Rezendes (from *Tracking & the Art of Seeing*, Camden House, 1992); page 22, J.D. Henry; page 23, Heather K. Lenz; page 24, J.D. Henry; page 26, AllStock/Art Wolfe; page 27, Wayne Lynch; page 28, AllStock/Art Wolfe

CHAPTER 2
page 32, First Light/Thomas Kitchin; page 33, First Light/Brian Milne; page 34, Animals Animals/Leonard Lee Rue III; page 35, First Light/Brian Milne; page 36, Tom Brakefield; page 37, J.D. Henry; page 38, First Light/John Sylvester; page 39, Paul Rezendes (from *Tracking & the Art of Seeing*, Camden House, 1992); page 40, J.D. Henry; page 41, J.D. Henry; page 42, First Light/Brian Milne; page 44, J.D. Henry; page 45, First Light/Thomas Kitchin; page 47, First Light/Brian Milne; page 48, First Light/Brian Milne; page 49, J.D. Henry; page 50, J.D. Henry; page 51, Bill Byrne; page 52, AllStock/J & M Ibbotson

CHAPTER 3
page 54, First Light/Brian Milne; page 56, left, Wayne Lynch; page 56, right, AllStock/Stephen Krasemann; page 57, J.D. Henry; page 58, First Light/Brian Milne; page59, J.D. Henry; page 61, J.D. Henry

CHAPTER 4
page 63, Bill Byrne; page 64, AllStock/Art Wolfe; page 65, J.D. Henry; page 66, Ron

Index